COMING HOME

SALLY NIXON HAINES

Sally Nixon Haines

COMING HOME

THE NORTH CAROLINA

OUTER BANKS

Tate Publishing & Enterprises

Published by Tate Publishing & Enterprises, LLC
127 E. Trade Center Terrace | Mustang, Oklahoma 73064 USA
1.888.361.9473 | www.tatepublishing.com

Tate Publishing is committed to excellence in the publishing industry. The company reflects the philosophy established by the founders, based on Psalm 68:11,
"The Lord gave the word and great was the company of those who published it."

Book design copyright © 2010 by Tate Publishing, LLC. All rights reserved.
Cover design by Leah LeFlore
Interior design by Stefanie Rooney

Published in the United States of America

ISBN: 978-1-61663-604-3
1. Travel, United States, South, South Atlantic (DC, DE, FL, GA, MD, NC, SC, VA, WV)
2. Biography & Autobiography, Personal Memoirs
10.06.10

DEDICATION

In memory of my father, who gave me a love of the Outer Banks, and for Aaron and Molly, who enabled me to remember its magic through a child's eyes.

This is also to acknowledge some of our visitors who "wrote" parts of this book.

TABLE OF CONTENTS

INTRODUCTION

There is a sliver of sand that extends itself into the sea beyond the usual coastline of North Carolina. Rich in pirate lore, ghost stories, nor'easters, and unpredictable weather, the Outer Banks continues to leave an indelible impression on those who are receptive.

Like most desirable beaches, this particularly vulnerable strip of sand has been overloaded with glitzy high-rise rentals, too many septic tanks, too many people, too much traffic, and too little patience. It's groaning under the weight, and greed tends to kill the "goose that laid the golden egg," but the beauty remains. You just have to look for it now.

The "Graveyard of the Atlantic" is partially illustrated by the remains of the *Laura A. Barnes* shipwreck in South Nags Head. The ship went down in

1921, and there was once a sign posted that explained the ship's history and urged visitors to "Take only photographs. Leave only footprints."

I recently talked with a friend who, like me, has experienced the Outer Banks for long periods of time over some years. Between the two of us, and many generations before and since, a lot of footprints have been lost, but high tide can't erase memories. This is for those who recall it from those years, as well as those generations, including our visitors, who followed and made their own footprints.

When you're at peace in your surroundings, you actually appreciate it at the time, and that's the difference. But it becomes even dearer when you realize it's being lost. Some people call that "just geography." I call that *Coming Home: The North Carolina Outer Banks,* and that's what this book is about.

Do leave footprints and take photographs. Don't forget to pack the memories when you leave.

NEVER
MAKE BROAD
GENERALIZATIONS
ABOUT PEOPLE

When I was growing up, my family spent many summer months in Nags Head on the Outer Banks. It was literally a family tradition. I felt I had returned home when I moved there in 1993, and upon arrival I found a dependable year-round job working as a reservationist for a real estate company that rents and manages vacation properties. Plus they paid benefits. I came to realize a sometimes mundane job can be quite interesting when you talk with a cross-section of people from all over the country, and I tried to appreciate the generalization rule as my parents advised. They taught me that when I made broad generalizations about people or situations, an exception would usually prove me wrong in the end.

After working in several aspects of real estate in different markets, this one was unique. There were many days when we were overwhelmed by the phones and forced to juggle back and forth between calls. In previous jobs I would have given my eye teeth for that kind of activity, and I tried to remember that when it seemed overwhelming. That, and the fact that the majority of the people calling us were endlessly patient when we were forced to put them on hold out of necessity.

The majority of our callers asked rational, intelligent questions about the Outer Banks. If our visitor had never been there before, there were considerably more questions, and that was expected. That was "Person A," and thankfully that type predominated, which gave one faith in mankind. But every now and then a "Person B" slipped in. Those were the ones who asked questions so unbelievable you wondered what they had been smoking! This led you to make broad generalizations like, "Type A is a rational human being" while "Type B doesn't have the brains of Jell-O."

Both Type A and Type B had more than likely saved all year to buy a week of serenity in the sun. You had to remind yourself of this with the Bs, especially with the Bs, because they could be trying. That type was obviously hurting for a big dose of serenity!

The most frequently asked question about a cottage under consideration was, "How far is it from the water?" Logical question. After all, the ocean is the main reason most of us assembled there in the first place. The best example of a Type B question: "What ocean is it on?" I told an associate about this, and she didn't skip a beat. Her immediate response: "What ocean do you want?" (Hey, we aimed to please.)

Type A questions often had to do with amenities included in the property under consideration. They were sensible questions like, "How do we find it? We've never been there before." There were also questions about bed sizes, baby furniture, things to do in the area, and how long a drive it was from Hampton Roads. Again, sensible questions. But the Type B questions fascinated me. They were the ones worth remembering because they were innovation at its best, creativity in its purest form. Example: the caller was given directions to the cottage she had reserved, and our rental assistant gave explicit directions, even down to the milepost signs that show up at expected intervals along the bypass (U.S. 158), to which she responded, "What is the distance between the mile posts?"

The Type Bs were fun, but the "Code 8s" were in a league all their own. One of our maintenance people came up with that one. Loosely defined, it means someone who had a lobotomy before breakfast.

I hadn't moved to the Outer Banks when the original Code 8 occurred, so this is hearsay. However, I was told this story by enough reliable people that I believed it and think it is worth passing on. One of our renters had called about his refrigerator, which wasn't cooling. He was asked the usual questions about his use of the appliance, and it was decided a maintenance person should be sent. When the repairman called our office to report, he described the situation as a Code 8. When asked, "What *is* a Code 8?" he responded, "I'll tell you when I get there."

As it turned out, our visitor had shoved a watermelon into his refrigerator that was so large the door wouldn't close. Little wonder the refrigerator wasn't cooling! And that was a Code 8, or at least a prime example of one.

I enjoyed those people I talked with daily, so if you are planning your first visit to the Outer Banks, here are a few tips that may make you more comfortable when you get there. For starters, Corolla on the northern Banks is not a car by Toyota, but rather a lovely place with predominantly high-end development. It is pronounced "ka-rah-la," not "ka-roll-a." However, if you have a four-wheel drive, you can drive a stretch north of Corolla where the road ends and the sand starts. It is pristinely beautiful, and the locals drove the wild ponies there to keep them safe. The natives and locals pronounce that area "ka-roll-a," and I personally think they do this to confuse people, but those shaggy horses aren't confused, so who's the smart one here? If you have a four-wheel drive and decide to explore the area, it's a good idea to go at low tide.

I first thought Rodanthe on Hatteras Island should be pronounced "Ro-danth" but the natives pronounce it "Ro-dan-thee." Don't ask me why, but I figured if they are from there, they can call it whatever they want, and they have a right to expect others to do the same.

Almost all housing on the banks is referred to as a "cottage," not a cabin or anything in between. Don't ask me why because I don't know. Personally, when I hear the term *cottage*, I envision a thatched roof and perennial garden in the English countryside. I realized how incongruous that term was during a conversation I had with a woman who had just reserved a rather expensive oceanfront property. At some point I mentioned her "cottage" because the term is natural to me. Immediate reaction: "Wait a minute! We're spending all this for a cottage?" I explained that was the local term, and it was definitely a misnomer for the glitzy property she had just rented. She seemed to feel comfortable with that once it was explained, and it was gorgeous. I'll bet she returned to it the following year.

The term *cottage* is a misnomer. It dates to those original grand matriarchs that dot the sand of Old Nags Head. Those were hardly cottages either by any stretch of the imagination. Jonathan Daniels, editor of *The Raleigh News and Observer* dubbed them "The Unpainted Aristocracy," which they are called to this day. It's perfect. "Cottage" is used to describe anything from the most humble abode to the ambitious "Hotel Californias" in Monterey Shores. I can't explain why. It just *is*.

The majority of our calls were from the northeast, but I reserved cottages for people calling from England and Germany as well. I locked in properties for a few Californians, but never one for Hawaii, although I did spot an "Aloha State" license plate in the Kmart parking lot once. That led me to wonder why someone from Hawaii would travel all the way to the Outer Banks to shop at Kmart.

• • •

I think human nature is complex and generally fascinating. Nowhere did we get a better slice of it than in our incoming calls. I remember the winter of '94 was not a happy time in the northeast, and it was especially gruesome for parts of Pennsylvania. I know this because I personally talked with every living Pennsylvanian over the age of twelve, and they all had one thing in common that winter: cabin fever. Those poor people were going nuts, understandably. I figured when the sound froze over on the Outer Banks, which is most unusual, it was unbearable there. The more it snowed in Pennsylvania, the more those folks dreamed of summer and the Outer Banks. I particularly remember one delightful man who was a schoolteacher by choice, not a "house husband." The schools were closed *forever*, so he and the children spent endless days at home while his wife managed to get to work. I think she took the snowplow. All considered, I thought he held up remarkably well because he only broke down twice during the course of our conversation.

I was intrigued by the diversity of accents I got on the phone. I attempted to figure out where our callers were from before I asked them. I got better and started listening for subtle differences, which often excludes New Jersey, but that one is interesting nevertheless. There is one group that always lets you know where they are calling from, first words out of their mouths, whether you want to know or not. (This is covered in a later chapter.)

I got an interesting "cabin" call once that really turned out to be a "cabin" call. He was calling from Iowa, which is no longer exceptional, since a number of our visitors come from that far away. Since he didn't have our brochure, I took his name and address so we could mail him one. Then I asked the usual questions: "When do you plan to come? How many are in your party?" When I told him about the first available cottage that showed up on my computer screen, he wanted to make sure it was in the Black Hills. My first thought was, *We've got Jockey's Ridge.* Then it hit me. I recalled, probably from a long-ago geography class, the Black Hills of South Dakota. So I asked him where he thought he was calling, and he replied, "South Dakota." When I told him he'd reached the Outer Banks of North Carolina, he was as incredulous as I. As it turned out, the toll-free number he meant to dial was exactly like ours with the exception of one digit.

He was a delightful person on the phone, very receptive, so I told him a bit about the banks and suggested he might want to think about taking his family there for vacation. He would have hardly have been the first person from Iowa to do that, and although I realized it was a long trip even when you flew, it seemed to be worth it to the people who did it. Otherwise they wouldn't return. He definitely seemed interested, and I have no idea of the outcome, but the brochure was mailed.

If I ever learned a lesson about not making broad generalizations about people, that was a prime example. Here was a guy calling for the Black Hills of South Dakota, and I introduced him to Jockey's Ridge, the highest sand dune on the east coast, and he got excited anyway. Nothing like hindsight to let you know your parents were right in the first place, which I of course hate to admit.

In talking with so many people, I realized there was one incongruity I couldn't figure out. How can there be such a marked difference between, say, a New York City accent accent and that of someone from upstate New York? Don't they all come from the same state? Here in North Carolina there is little difference between a Greenville and Fayettville accent, for example; although, now that I consider this, I have found two rather distinctive dialects in North Carolina. One is the northeastern North Carolina "Tidewater" dialect, which I can't convey phonetically, but you hear it clearly in words like *around*, *down*, and *town*.

Once you hear the second dialect, you will never forget it. It is that of the true Outer Banks native, the product of generations there on the banks with origins in England. For lack of a better term, I call it an *Elizabethan brogue*. It is incomparable, and I love it. There was a time that was about all you heard, but today it seems to have been almost silenced. The Outer Banks has become a melting pot, a microcosm of America, and that may be healthy. But I do miss that brogue.

I may have missed a distinctive North Carolina mountain dialect, and if so, I apologize. I make it a practice to stay away from the mountains because they make me seasick. No joke. I have never been seasick on the water, even under widely varying conditions, but the mountains make me seasick. There is no other term to describe that queasy feeling I get rounding mountain curves, and it doesn't matter who's driving. I could be driving, and it makes no difference. I have always felt lightheaded and sleepy in the mountains, which is no doubt the result of the change in altitude. If I want that feeling, I figure I could go buy a stiff drink, which is a lot cheaper than the price of gas to get me from Manteo to Murphy.[1]

I just hope this mountain talk doesn't offend the North Carolina Department of Tourism. After all, they are selling the Great Smokey Mountains too, and I definitely don't want to get on the bad side of those folks.

Of course I *personally* have absolutely no discernable accent, even though I was born and reared in the South. I've gathered some people don't think this is the case, so you'll just have to take my word for it.

GOD'S COUNTRY, USA

My love of the Outer Banks was first nurtured by carefree childhood summers spent next to the ocean's edge in "Old Nags Head." Back then there was always sand between my toes, a bit of wind at my back, the sun's warmth on my face, and the water—always the water—within reach. That part has never changed. The outward appearance of the Outer Banks has changed dramatically in my lifetime, but that part doesn't change. And the beauty is, that special place is passed from generation to generation. We never really own it because after all, that is God's country, but we are allowed to be there, derive strength from it, and share it with those we love.

These are my perceptions only. I especially enjoyed hearing other perceptions from different parts of the country. Every now and then when I would have preferred not to go to work, I remembered some of the conversations and the people I talked with, and that made the day worth showing up for. Those are the people who take something memorable home and leave only footprints. Those people went back. They always returned, and I loved talking with them.

I once had a conversation with a woman from the Cleveland area who was addicted to the Outer Banks. She and her family found their place in the sun there about ten years ago, and they have returned ever since for their annual vacation. When she called to rent a cottage, she related a great story. Back home, she was walking past the TV set on the way to fold laundry and overheard what she first thought was a car ad. For whatever reason, the announcer stated, "And the *best* beach on the east coast is the Outer Banks." When she heard that, she dropped the laundry basket, gave her television the thumbs up, and literally screamed at the set, "Yes! Yes!" while she jumped up and down. She then admitted she was embarrassed by this outburst just afterward because her children, who were watching a program, looked at her like she was nuts. I told her I thought she was about the sanest person I had talked with in some time and predicted her children would ultimately scream at their own TVs, given sufficient exposure to the Outer Banks.

I got a thought-provoking call from a woman in New Jersey. She had spent her childhood summers next to the ocean, and although her ocean was colder than mine, the end result was the same. She became hooked on the water. She spent most of her adult life near the water, and like me, she moved away at one point and went through a sort of withdrawal as a result. She is now close to the water again, as I am, and she posed an interesting question. She wondered if being introduced to, and repeatedly exposed to the water at an early age made a difference. She asked if people with that experience had a different perspective from the general population. She had no answer, nor did I.

Some time after that conversation, I was taking an inventory of one of our rentals and discovered a statement framed on a bedroom wall that seemed to have a bearing on this. I thought it was worth repeating. Draw your own conclusions:

> "All of us have in our veins the exact same percentage of salt that exists in the ocean, and therefore we have salt in our blood, in our sweat, and in our tears. We are tied to our oceans, and when we go back to sea ... whether to sail it or to watch it ... we are going back to whence we came."

This quote captured the essence of the Outer Banks, and I've never forgotten it for that reason. That, and because the person who penned it was John F. Kennedy.

• • •

Once I answered a call and got a gentleman with an intriguing accent. He began by stating, "I'm calling from Frankfurt, Germany." All I could think to say was, "Welcome to the Outer Banks!" This was hardly the first call we had gotten from overseas, but I tended to make an assumption about calls like this. These people were dead serious about going there when they pay top-dollar for that sort of long-distance call and can't access our toll-free lines, plus they have to call us during our business hours. My German friend had a beautiful command of the English language. As it turned out, he was a senior executive with Lufthansa Airlines and discovered the banks about ten years ago. It was then he started flying his family there for vacation, which is additional proof one should not make broad generalizations about people, because I always assumed Germans vacationed on the Mediterranean, or at least on the Rhine. We fixed him right up.

The happiest aspect of that business was the fact that most of those who dialed our number were upbeat in anticipation of their vacation, and I find it reinforcing to talk with happy people. *Ecstatic* would be more accurate in terms of much of the northeast, based on the winter of '94!

Every now and then I got a true sense of humor. A woman called to inform me, "My dog needs a vacation." She wanted a cottage that allowed pets, and we had those. My first thought was, *Is this woman for real?* Indeed she was, and she made my day. She only addressed her dog's needs as she made the reservation, sticking with the dog story throughout our conversation. Once I learned she had a Lab (Labrador retriever), we truly spoke the same language. Now that I think about it, *I* would have reserved a week at the beach for a Lab.

One of my most memorable calls was from a woman in Washington State. She spent most of her childhood summers on the Outer Banks and continued to be connected. She returned every chance she could. She was very close to her mother, who spent her summers there as a child many years ago, just as my father did back before the area was discovered by the rest of the world. In this call, my friend from Washington lined up and paid for a cottage for her mother and herself. Her mother had chosen it from our brochure, and she knew precisely what she wanted. "Old Nags Head," or as close to it as she could get because that's where it all started, and she remembered that. Her mother wanted a plain, simple cottage on the ocean because that's the way it was when she lived it. Old Nags Headers tend to be that way, and their requirements are basic. They want no more than a decent roof over their heads, some truly fresh seafood, and the waves lapping at their toes. *Her mother got it.*

This turned out to be the saddest call I'd gotten. The daughter lined up the no-frills oceanfront cottage for her mother because her mother was dying. All she wanted was one last visit to the place she called home.

I frequently referred to the banks as "God's country" when I talked with our callers because I believe it is, but it is encouraging to have your beliefs reinforced by others occasionally. I remember a family in our office picking up keys to their vacation home. I was on the phone, and someone else was helping them. During the phone conversation, I must have made a reference to "God's country," and the father of the family obviously overheard this. As they were walking out the door after I hung up, he turned to me and said, "You are absolutely right. This is God's country!"

If you doubt this, don't take my word for it. Ask some of the old troopers who knew it years ago at its pristine best. Talk with those who pack fond memories to take home. Better yet, ask God where he would go on vacation, if he ever could get some time off.

VIRGINIA—THE
LEAST COMMON
OF ALL THE
"WEALTHS"

I know this seems an odd title for a chapter on the Outer Banks, but read on. I expect you will get my drift.

If you are going to the Outer Banks for the first time, you will quickly realize there are at least as many Virginians there as North Carolinians. I have personally conducted a *highly scientific* survey while driving in summer traffic on the bypass (Route 158), applying makeup in my rearview mirror, and my study revealed that Virginia license plates outnumber North Carolina plates by a significant number. (A bunch.) And that does not include those Virginia transplants who, like me, were finally forced to shell out a ton of money to buy North Carolina plates or go to jail. This defies analysis because what you've got, folks, is a whole slew of Virginians driving around with North Carolina plates, sort of like Virginians in drag.

This scientific study does not accurately reflect the fact that there are more vanity license plates per capita in Virginia than from all the rest of the states put together. Nor does this even begin to take into account the annual ritual of "Beach Week," whereupon every Virginian under the age of twenty-one feels compelled to come crashing onto the Outer Banks as soon as school is out in order to "vent."

I had not personally analyzed this Beach Week phenomenon, but I knew the ratio of increased boom boxes, deck beer parties, and lean, tan thighs grew in direct proportion to the migraine headaches of the police departments and property owners and managers up and down the beach. Actually this one defies analysis! But once Beach Week was over and the trash was cleaned up, the Outer Banks settled back into being the family beach it always was.

If you are visiting the Outer Banks from somewhere other than Virginia, I thought it might be helpful for you to have some hot tips on the "Virginia mentality," since you will probably encounter a lot of it on the Outer Banks. I am a native Virginian, so I conclude I'm in as good a position as anybody to give you the scoop on this. Now isn't this better than *Europe on the Cheap?* Those people never give you the actual scoop. They may excel at telling you what a bed and breakfast will cost you in Austria, but they never give you the *real dirt,* the very facts enquiring minds want to know.

• • •

There are some types of constructive criticism I find valid. The one that tops my list is this: it is perfectly okay to analyze, even criticize, the state where you were born, especially if you lived there long enough to get on the local tax rolls, but for less time than it took to get a copy of your birth certificate back from the state capital. I was born in Virginia and lived there for years. I love Virginia, but it can come across as "Camelot with an attitude." This is a prime example: Virginia is not a state in the first place. It's a commonwealth, and there aren't many of those kicking around in our union, but Virginia is, and believe me, it is the least common of all the "wealths"! So for the curious minds in the crowd, here is your scoop on Virginia:

1.   A primary rule of thumb with most Virginians is they have "a sense of history."

     Or at least those over the age of twenty-one do. Never underestimate this concept when dealing with a Virginian because any Virginian worth his salt will ultimately reveal that he is a "direct descendant" of Thomas Jefferson.

If you are from Ohio or Pennsylvania, for example, you might well ask, "So what?" Valid question. In order to understand this you need to realize that in Virginia, on a scale of one to ten, God gets an eleven, and Thomas Jefferson gets a 10.98. So what we've got here is a commonwealth simply splitting at the seams with "direct descendants" of Thomas Jefferson, if you are to believe all these people. The next logical question would be, "What did Jefferson *really* do in his spare time? How one man with no serious history of promiscuity could father so many "direct descendants" beats me. After all, we are not talking about Casanova here!

2. Second rule of thumb: Virginia is "The mother of presidents."

Last time I counted, Virginia had produced more presidents than any other state or commonwealth. There were seven or eight, but you can't trust my numbers because I tend to round up. Anyway, this president thing is a point of pride in the commonwealth.

3. Third rule of thumb: It is very important that you manage to "Be born in Virginia" if you ever aspire to be a lead dog. After all, "if you ain't the lead dog, the scenery never changes." Case in point: Charles Robb, a former governor and U.S. Senator from Virginia, encountered a problem with that very situation. In one of Robb's earliest campaigns, there was a

television ad featuring his mother's statement that she "would have crossed the Potomac" to give birth to her son in Virginia, if only she had realized "how important it was." Big mistake, lady. You almost blew it for your son before he was born.

4. Now if you really want to get a handle on Virginia, there are two terms you are going to have to master. *The University* is one of them. If you drive through Virginia on the way to the Outer Banks, you may see a profusion of car window decals which simply state "*The* University." If you happen to be from out of state and haven't the foggiest notion which university they are referring to, it is of course *The* University of Virginia, which was of course founded by Thomas Jefferson, who is turning out to be about the swingingest founding father we had, if you are to believe all his "direct descendants."

5. As we've now discovered, when Jefferson wasn't founding universities, he was founding "FFVs" or "first families of Virginia." It could include the governor, but it might not. Virginians are very democratic that way. If the governor adheres to the old Harry Byrd pay-as-you-go philosophy and went to the "right" schools, he could be a contender for FFV, but that is no absolute guarantee. The actual litmus test boils down to: "Yes, but do we know his family?"

FFVs can be old money and frequently are, but the common thread is the family history, which traces its roots to a great-great-granddad—usually granddaddy Beauregard Jefferson—who lived out his incredibly genteel life on the banks of the James and founded lots of "direct descendants," which in itself, is a *very Virginian* thing to do, especially after a few mint juleps.

If you are planning to visit the Outer Banks, it may be helpful for you to know right up front that you will probably encounter many of these simply marvelous Virginia genes oozing themselves onto the banks. If you don't believe me, you are free to conduct your own scientific survey of license plates.

North Carolinians are used to this mentality, take it in stride, and go on about their business. On those rare occasions when a North Carolinian gets pushed too far by all this genetic perfection, he may ultimately mutter something about North Carolina being "a valley of humility between two mountains of conceit." I never understood how this statement applied to South Carolina, except maybe Charleston, but it often seems to apply to Virginia. When a North Carolinian is finally pushed to this point, he usually utters the statement quietly, so the offender won't be offended. North Carolinians tend to be very polite that way, and I know this because I grew up in North Carolina, so I also know there are times it just feels good to say it.

In spite of all this, I do love Virginia. *What Is It About Virginia?* is a Virginia classic written by Guy Friddell, who wrote for *The Virginian-Pilot* for years. It is one of my all-time favorite books because it eloquently captures the essence of Virginia, the beauty of the land, the people at their best, and the history. I size it up this way. If you were born in Virginia and spent a good part of your life there, it is not so different from breaking in a new pair of good shoes. There may be resistance at first, but over time good shoes become comfortable, enduring, indispensable. Those are the ones you can't bring yourself to throw away, so they end up sitting there occupying prime top shelf space because it's nice to open your closet on a rainy morning and find an old friend. Being from Virginia is a lot like that.

So you folks sitting there in traffic and heat and exhaust fumes between Hampton Roads and the banks might want to conduct your own license plate survey. It is not a bad diversion. Hey, anything to beat the heat!

The good news is that additional bridges have worked wonders to alleviate the old bottleneck effect and speed the flow considerably. The bad news is that the next chapter is also about Virginia.

"I'M CALLING FROM_____"

At the time I worked for the real estate company, we got well over 3,000 calls per month about vacation rental property on the Outer Banks. My experience was that out of all those calls, there was only *one city* whose residents consistently introduced themselves by beginning, "I'm calling from_____." There were many people from all over who began their conversations that way, and that was fine. We wanted to know where they were calling from and usually asked if they didn't volunteer it.

The difference was, that particular city always introduced itself that way as if to let me know: "Forewarned is forearmed." I can't recall one exception in all of my talks with that crowd. Just after the introduction, the demands normally followed, and the first one was predictable. "We *must* have oceanfront." Just after that the list of requirements kicked in, and those people never stopped long enough to learn that the oceanfront cottages were all taken months ago and, "For crying out loud, what do you expect when you call in mid-June thinking you are going to lock in your dream vacation two weeks hence? Not only do we not have oceanfront, we don't have anything left at all during peak season, so stick that one in your ditty bag. Ha-ha!" Of course you couldn't say that, but even if you could, it wouldn't have mattered because they didn't hear a thing until the requirements were completed and they stopped to gasp for breath. Once the reality sank in, most of them found that "very disappointing." That bunch disappoints easily. When you attempted to help them deal with their disappointment, many of them repeated their original introductory sentence, "I'm calling from_____," as if they expected that fact to alter reality. It didn't. Besides it was redundant because you already knew where they were calling from and that was *before* they told you the first time. That particular accent is so recognizable in the first two or three syllables uttered that you were tempted to cut them off midstream in the first sentence to say, "Yes I know, you are calling from *Richmond*." But of course you couldn't do that either.

I now refer to one of my favorite Richmond calls as the "lounghe" chair call, and this is one of my favorites because it is so typically "Richmond." (For the benefit of those who aren't familiar with "Richmond-speak," *lounghe* is lounge, for example. Southern syr-upy is considered charming in some circles, and there were several examples from our caller.)That was a woman caller who was obviously out of touch with reality. For starters, I'd be willing to bet that woman didn't believe for one minute that the South lost the Civil War. She didn't want to refight it because she never realized the South lost in the first place! The dreams of the genteel grandeur of the "ohld" (old) South were as alive to that woman as they were to her grandmother who, no doubt, referred to the Civil War as "The Late Unpleasantness." I always think it helps to know where this sort of person is com-ing from, right up front. In the case of Richmond, I suspect it could be a time warp problem.

Our "lounghe" chair example began by telling me where she was calling from. She then told me, "We must have oceanfront, of course," and she said, "of course," which really makes her a prime exam-ple. Next step, the requirements kicked in. In this instance, our grande dame called in May rather than June, so there was something left, but it definitely wasn't oceanfront, and she was, predictably, "very disappointed."

Calls from Richmond women were almost never short. I got ten minutes of "disappointment" before the next list of demands set in. Those mainly had to do with "ahmenities" (amenities). The list was end-less, and all the while we were being slammed with incoming calls and this woman was tying up one of our toll-free lines. After a number of requirements were met, she finally made a reservation, and that should have been the end of it. It wasn't.

Act Two: This is our "lounghe" chair segment, which required several more calls. "Are there *lounghe* chairs on the property?" I explained if lounghe chairs weren't mentioned in the property description in our brochure, she could assume there would be no lounghe chairs. This was "particularly disappointing," but she brightened considerably once I told her about the "perfectly *mahvelous* (marvelous) local rental companies, which supply everything under the sun, *but especially lounghe chairs,* and these lovely people will deliver them to your very doorstep if you give them a little advance notice." If you live in Virginia long enough, you learn to do "Richmond-speak" in self-defense. At that point our friend was beginning to get very comfortable with this lounghe chair delivery concept, particularly after I gave her their toll-free number, which freed up ours.

Act Three: "How many can I seat at the table?" I explained she could seat the number stated in our brochure by the maximum occupancy described for the cottage she'd reserved. After the second or third seating call, my gut response was, "Lady, I *don't care!* Seat as many as you want. Does anyone in your crowd have a large lap? Great! Pile one on top of the other at one place setting, and load up the plate. Big plate. Seat them on the floor. Throw a doggie bag their way. *Get a grip, lady. You are coming to the beach, not giving an inaugural dinner party!*" Naturally I couldn't say that either, but I was left with a nagging sense that that sort of mentality had a lot to do with the South losing the Civil War.

Next thing you know, I overheard one of my coworkers talking with someone who was obviously asking multiple questions about the color scheme of the cottage under consideration. Now I ask you, why would anyone be concerned about the color scheme of a privately owned cottage when all that person plans to do is vacation there for one week out of fifty-two? Is that person coming to redecorate? When my coworker got off the phone, I couldn't resist, so I asked her where her caller was from. I'll let you figure out the answer to that one.

Richmond men are not very different from their female counterparts. The basic conversation had all of the same ingredients. The only discernable difference I found was that most men from Richmond tended to be "very busy," which was a great concept because they rarely tied up your toll-free lines for long.

• • •

I believe when you visit a place you should make an attempt to apply that old adage, "When in Rome, do as the Romans do." This is a loose adaptation of the original phrase, but the point is clear. Don't impose your cultural standards on the place you are visiting; be it Europe, Asia, Africa, or even the Outer Banks. If you don't give a hoot about the other culture, why leave home in the first place?

If you are going there for the first time, you're

not expected to know the local terms, and that's fine. However, if you've been going there since two days before sand and know the lay of the land, as many of our Richmond "ambassadors" did, you should know *they are not "cabins"!* The bloody structures are *cottages,* and yes, *cottage* may be a misnomer, but *cabin* is too for that matter. I suppose I subscribe to that old Roman philosophy because I learned about the Roman Empire well before I learned about the Richmond Empire.

I have some good friends in Richmond who are delightful people, so I'm sure there must be any number of delightful people in that city, but I can remember first wondering about that crowd when I lived in Hampton Roads. That's where they invaded Virginia Beach. When it was time to leave, they talked about going "back to town" as they left a city with well over one and a half million people.

So I worried about Richmond, and I finally decided part of its problem was the fact that it didn't have a decent body of water close at hand. I thought it did at first because I'd always heard, "Richmond sits on the James," so I envisioned Richmond sitting on this mighty river. And the James is an impressive river in many places, but when it piddles its way through Richmond, it is little more than a dried-up streambed with a bunch of rocks poking out. That concerned me, so I decided the best therapy for Richmond would be a weekend in Norfolk. You know, rent a room at the Omni on the waterfront, kick back, and watch an aircraft carrier navigate a tight 180-degree turn in the Elizabeth River. That sight moves the landscape and boggles the mind. For receptive types, the spectacle ultimately nourishes the soul.

Since experiencing Richmond on the Outer Banks, I'm not sure even an aircraft carrier could move that mentality! Because I love my native commonwealth, I find it hard to believe "The mother of presidents" could have produced the mother of all cities, so I told myself Richmond probably arrived full-blown on the scene when Virginia wasn't paying attention and had its back turned. I concluded Virginia must have been out of pocket at the time; you know, out doing all the stuff Virginia does best, like composing the Declaration of Independence and "First Families of Virginia." It was at that very moment Richmond slipped in the back door, got a toehold, and started suffocating like kudzu. Next thing you know, Virginia got back home, primed the pump, and discovered … Richmond.

Now that we have covered this subject in depth, it's time to return to the twenty-first century.

LIFE IN THE
FAST LANE

Just when I thought I had a handle on where people were coming from, someone slipped in a call that knocked my socks off. This was a call from a fellow who wanted to know what there was "to do" on the Outer Banks.

We were frequently asked that question by first-time visitors, and we usually tried to learn more about our callers before suggesting possible activities. Did they have children? If so, how old were the children? People with young children seeking sun, sea, and solitude would often be told about Duck and Corolla. For those with teenagers, the Nags Head, Kill Devil Hills, and Kitty Hawk area was a natural because teens usually wanted to find other teens, walk to a fishing pier, or at least have a 7–11 or shopping center within reach so they didn't go through complete withdrawal. Young couples renting a cottage for a week's getaway from the children might want the nightlife that abounds from Nags Head to Kitty Hawk. In this instance I told them about several good spots and then suggested they take the Pub Crawl, those wonderful beach buses with the open-air seating level on top, which once ran on the Outer Banks. They looked like a lot more fun than riding in the back seat of a police car. The police are vigilant about DUIs there! Family reunion groups generally wanted to know where they could buy the most food for less, and honeymooners were the easiest of all. All they required was a hot tub and each other. But there was one thing they all had in common: "Where can we go to eat great seafood?" which conclusively proves my theory that most people travel on their stomachs.

As it turned out, my caller from the fast lane was bringing several other couples, plus children, varying in ages from toddler to teen, so I had a wide-open field. I liked that best. The biggest challenge in that instance was condensing several lifetimes of activity in a brief telephone conversation.

I started with water-related activities. Aside from swimming, body boarding, and surfing, there are jet skis, power boats, sailboats, catamarans, kayaks, canoes, wave runners, and wind surfers available almost anywhere up and down that stretch of sand. In fact, Hatteras Island has a particular body of water that is an ideal wind surfing spot that is well known as "The Canadian Hole" because it attracts so many Canadians, as well as wind surfers from up and down the east coast. There are water parks and the aquarium where "Jaws" lives in Manteo, as well as some of the best surf-casting and deep-sea fishing to be found anywhere in the world. There once was a sign posted in Duck that described it well, "We Are Serious about Your Fun."

"The Land Where Flight Began" offers airplane and seaplane tours, and there is hang gliding for the free spirits in the crowd. I personally think if Wilbur and Orville Wright visited today, they would opt for that and a kite, plus, of course, a tour in a plane.

There is golf and tennis for the "landlubbers." Hiking trails abound in beautiful settings, and you can take a horseback ride on the beach, climb the stairs of a lighthouse, or visit the Elizabethan Gardens. Definitely visit the Wright Brothers National Memorial. There are nature tours, dolphin tours, and at the other end of the spectrum there is go-kart racing.

The Lost Colony is a *must*—don't leave the banks without it. If your children are with you, by all means include them in this adventure because the children love it best. Created by Paul Green, the Pulitzer Prize-winning playwright, it is not only the first symphonic play ever produced in America, but is also the longest running outdoor drama. Many actors, such as Andy Griffith, got their start performing in *The Lost Colony*. It is staged on the very spot where the original event took place over 400 years ago. Spend an evening under the stars with your children. This pageant packs more punch than Barney and MTV combined, but don't take my word for it. Ask the children who have experienced it. Better yet, watch your own child during an "Indian attack" on the banks of the Roanoke Sound.

I told my fast lane caller about some of this, and I included an overview of the great places to eat and shop there. I may have mentioned the outlet mall in South Nags Head and, given his disposition, I probably mentioned some of the local watering holes. Knowing me, I no doubt mentioned Tommy's Market in Duck, where you can pick up any newspaper worth reading in the western hemisphere, plus wonderful angus beef and one of the best gourmet food selections I've found.

At the end of my litany of special effects for Fast Lane and his group, he responded: "I don't think we'll go there. Not enough action." Not "enough action"? Who did this guy think he was anyway, Donald Trump? What was this person's problem? What did he want, and after all, how big a bite can you take out of one week's slice of life?

Did he want casinos? Hey, we aimed to please. They had Bingo up and down the beach, and I heard they got a really good bingo crowd on Wednesday nights at the Colington Fire Station. After all, how good can it get?

All kidding aside, I spent some time thinking about this, and I worry about people like Fast Lane. Thankfully, there are no casinos on the Outer Banks, and that's the last thing that place needs. But Fast Lane apparently had a real need to live on the cutting edge, so I finally figured out a great vacation spot for this guy. It doesn't have casinos either, but I suspect it may have enough gusto to satisfy him for up to one week. Unfortunately by the time I thought of it he had hung up, so I'll tell you about it instead in the next chapter.

WEEKEND
FROM HELL

Anyone with the sophistication of a soybean has better sense than to fall for a timeshare promo weekend,
right? Wrong! It all depends on who presents it to
you.

If it comes in the form of a slick telephone call
at the dinner hour, you already know you have about
three options. (You may not have thought of the
third one, but it really is the most fun.)

Option 1. Slam the phone down real hard.

Option 2. Listen briefly, then hit them with
the same words you used the last time you
untangled the Christmas tree lights.

Option 3. My personal favorite: If you're a
typical family with a smart telephone, ask the

caller to hold while you pretend to go find the "decision maker" in the family. At this point, you simply put the phone down, push the "speaker" button and go eat your dinner. This may be against the law, but I'll swear it's worth it. You wouldn't believe what those telemarketing experts say as they wait for someone to come to the phone.

Everyone in our family, including the dog, knew better than to fall for that sort of "incredible time-share opportunity," but it's a different story when a coworker asks: "How would you and your husband like a free weekend in a condo on the oceanfront at Myrtle Beach?" This was before moving to the Outer Banks, so I responded, "Is the pope a Catholic?" This coworker was an up front sort of person, and she told me straight out that as timeshare owners she and her husband would get fifty dollars for each prospect they sent. She was very candid about the presentation we'd have to sit through because she was like that. It had been a long winter, so we figured that would be a fair trade, ninety minutes of hard sell in exchange for a weekend in the sun on the beach.

Lisa called to confirm our reservation and get our hundred-dollar refundable deposit. She was so enthusiastic about our oceanfront stay that I liked her immediately and was looking forward to meeting her. Unfortunately, she wasn't there when we arrived quite late on Friday night, which was mainly due to the fact that Lisa's directions weren't particularly helpful.

When we finally reached our destination on the oceanfront, we met a very nice fellow who was stuck with the night shift. He was probably being paid minimum wage to tell expectant people like us that we weren't really staying on the oceanfront but somewhere near a golf course about five miles away. His directions were better than Lisa's, even down to "If you go past the Chevrolet dealership on the right, you've gone too far." It was easy to find. There was a huge golf ball the size of a water tower just before the entrance, and the security measures appeared to be first rate. We had to unlock a number of gates and doors before we discovered no filters for the coffee maker and twin beds.

We had been assured we could use the condo's facilities on the oceanfront, or at least park near them if we could find a place, and we planned to do exactly that the next morning. That was before we found out about "Bikers' Week." This is no joke, and I kid people a lot, but even in my wildest imaginings I could not have dreamed up the annual week-long convention of the National Bikers' Association in Myrtle Beach, South Carolina. If you ever had a fantasy about seeing a real live Hells Angel up close and personal, there were about 40,000 of them present for you to choose from that weekend. Apparently they roar down from all over America, and the Harleys predominate, but it's interesting to see yuppie types on Yamahas too. The whole crowd seemed to speak the same language. Maybe they divided into subgroups after buying T-shirts and beer. I was irritated with myself for not knowing about this compelling national event, but I was even more irritated when getting to the beach proved to be more trouble than it was worth.

It's taken me a long time to learn it's better for your blood pressure level not to get overly angry, so I try to get philosophical instead, which led me to wonder why one of the groups referred to itself as the "Scorpion Club." Next, I wondered if the Myrtle Beach Department of Economic Development purposely tried to encourage the bikers' annual weekend, and if so, how did they handle riot control?

When we showed up for our timeshare presentation, we found magic parking and were left to mill around with bad coffee and other invited guests on the sixth floor of the condo we had all been promised but never got. It overlooked the most pristine stretch of beach I'd seen in years, with only a sheet of plate glass to stop us from riding a wave or stretching out on the sand. If a marketing plan ever went awry, it was this one. They dragged us from God's portfolio to a small, dark cubicle where we overheard the couple in the next booth. We gathered, by bits and pieces, that this couple lived in a trailer park, and they appeared to be selling their souls to recapture what they had discovered in each other before the kids. They clearly couldn't afford it; we learned that much through the walls, but they were encouraged to sign the papers anyway. We didn't know the outcome, but we suspected they took more baggage home than they brought, in spite of the spectacular view just outside, which they were never allowed to touch.

As for us, we didn't meet Lisa, but we got our deposit back and probably set a record for shortening a ninety-minute sales presentation to fifteen minutes. I concluded our sales representative was absolutely perfect for selling timeshare plans since a basic shampoo and passing SAT score were obviously not part of his job description. He appeared to be mortgaging his soul to shortchange dreams so he could live well.

I'd originally described this as our Weekend from Hell because of the bikers. Now that I've had time to think about it, I'd opt for tattoos and the Scorpion Club any day over impossible dreams peddled by a pathetic figure in a polyester suit. But I would be willing to bet Fast Lane has already bought his own timeshare there by now. Perfect match!

ONLY THIRTY-EIGHT COTTAGES ON THE BEACH

A simple watercolor once hung just inside the main door to my father's cottage in Old Nags Head. The original colors were so muted by time that the surrounding pine frame almost overshadowed it. In spite of the passage of years, the artist's intent worked through the layers to reveal two lonely cottages perched defiantly on pilings, their shingle-clad coats mellowed by sun and wind and salt air. The massive high-pitched roofs reached down to shelter long porches and the generations of lives who grew up and grew young there and learned to love the sea. When I first noticed this watercolor, my father told me he could remember when there were only thirty-eight cottages on the beach. He would know. His childhood summers were spent in one of those matriarchal ancient cottages securely planted next to the ocean.

My grandmother sold the summer home when her sons left for World War Two. Her husband had died long before, but she held onto it for years after that, mainly for the children, but also for her private memories there with him, I suspect. Once the boys left, the sale was inevitable. I have come to realize there was a sad finality about the sale of that place, like an era ended, a childhood finished.

Her children later said in jest they never forgave her for selling the summer place, but of course they did. One would forgive my grandmother anything, although I cannot imagine her requiring forgiveness. She had an absolute passion for fairness and an inherent dignity that cannot be learned. Although my grandmother knew the Bible by rote, I never was convinced she believed the verse from Matthew that advised against building your house on sand. My grandmother was not a foolish woman. In her day there was no dune line to obstruct the water's flow because Old Nags Headers knew the sand dunes could not keep the ocean out once it decided to come in. Back then, smart sand builders worked with nature by building on pilings over flat sand so the ocean could occasionally roll underneath to vent its fury and hopefully return to its original resting place. In fact, my father told me they had a small dinghy that was kept under the cottage for just such occasions. Nor'easters were a great source of entertainment then, and when a good blow pushed the water in, he and his siblings would hop in the boat and ride the tide from the back of the cottage all the way behind to Jockey's Ridge. He described it as quite a ride! The wind from a nor'easter can be quite impressive, so if the wind came from the right direction, the kids all got serving trays from the kitchen and held them over their heads to catch the wind as they ran across the long front porch. The only problem occurred when my father's youngest brother, who was fairly small and lightweight then, was blown over the railing on the end of the porch and landed in the sand below. He was slightly scratched and couldn't wait to do it again, so all things considered, he got the best "ride" of all!

My grandmother knew about building smart on sand, and after many years of weathering storms on the oceanfront, the old place still stands today as testimony to that building code concept. I don't know how my grandmother worked it out with Matthew, who advised us to build our house on a rock, but knowing her, she did it with dignity.

My father was a firm believer in the Bible, but he also took issue with Matthew when it came to building on sand. This is the man who was solely responsible for bringing my brother and me full circle in terms of the Outer Banks. Even though my brother and I grew up on the North Carolina mainland, miles away from the banks, our father brought his childhood memories alive for us with his bedtime stories, which almost always began, "When I was a little boy at Nags Head ... " As soon as we heard that introduction, we knew we were in for a great story and would snuggle under the covers in anticipation.

The true stories of his summer childhood were the best, but they were sometimes enhanced by tales of real land pirates who stalked Jockey's Ridge with a nag and a lantern to lead unwary sailors to a shallow grave just beyond the breakers. Sailors at sea would spot the lantern hung from the neck of a horse led by a land pirate up and down Jockey's Ridge and assume it was the light of a sailing vessel sitting at anchor in a safe harbor. Big mistake! When they sailed to this "friendly port," they usually ended shipwrecked on the shallow shoals of the Graveyard of the Atlantic and the land pirates rowed out to capture the bounty.

If our attention waned, which it rarely did, he would throw in an occasional Outer Banks ghost story. As a result of those bedtime stories, nor'easters pounded our windows and land pirates stalked our backyard, light years away from that fragile strip of sand.

Our father's stories became my own children's favorite stories as well. They remained so vivid in my memory that when I recalled them for my children, I would often inadvertently begin, "When I was a little boy at Nags Head ... " at which point they would remind me I was their mom and had never been a little boy! Nevertheless, those were the stories they requested, and I loved watching them respond, just as my brother and I had years ago. The Outer Banks has a way of connecting generations.

Dad taught us to swim almost as soon as we learned to walk. There was no better coach. Not only did he teach swimming when he was a Naval officer, but—this is the part I'm not supposed to tell—he also dove off the flight deck of an aircraft carrier and survived to tell my brother and me about it in a weak moment years later. (Maybe the decks were closer to the water in those days. I don't know.) I expect if the Surgeon General had been up to speed in those days he would have issued a warning against such foolhardy ventures, at least for normal people. Our father would have been exempt from such a warning because he was not "normal" in that regard. He was part dolphin. We are all mammals, and I figure some dolphin genes got mixed in somewhere, and once dolphins connect with the sea, they are in control of their environment, even sharks to some extent. This could account for the perpetual smiles you find on the faces of porpoises and their cousins, and if that isn't something to smile about, I can't imagine what is.

By the time our parents built the summer place where the waves licked our heels, my brother and I had been thoroughly coached during previous summers there to take on the Atlantic Ocean. I came to love taking an early morning "dip" with him, as he called it. If that involved getting beyond the massive breakers of a true nor'easter for a good, clean swim just beyond, he had prepared us. The dolphin took riptides quite seriously, and he carefully taught us about the occasional perverse nature of the Grave-yard of the Atlantic. I would rather have faced a serious riptide than my father's wrath if I mishandled one, which may account for the fact that I'm alive to talk about riptides. The dolphin first taught us immense respect for the ocean. The love came later, but it is enduring, which leads me to believe I may have inherited a few dolphin genes of my own.

Some years ago the family was at the Nags Head place, and we took the bypass to go out to dinner. My father was appalled at the traffic on a weeknight in the late fall on the Outer Banks. He couldn't believe anyone would travel such a distance to drive in what he perceived to be "heavy" traffic. We then talked about where the traffic was coming from: New York, Philadelphia, D.C. I told him I assumed that traffic looked like a bit of heaven to our visitors, not to mention the natural amenities.

Dolphins are normally a chatty breed, but he got very quiet at that point, which was unusual for him. I can't be sure, but I sensed he was recalling a time when there was no Beach Road and no bypass, back when his family made the trip there by boat when there was no running water or electricity. I remember from my own childhood when there was no bypass and the Beach Road had been erased by the Ash Wednesday storm. That was years ago. His memories must have seemed eons ago in comparison, those long-ago summers when there were only thirty-eight cottages on the beach.

I like his memories best.

FISHERMEN, COME AS YOU ARE

Saint Andrew's-by-the-Sea Episcopal Church has been an Outer Banks landmark for many years. Originally built near Roanoke Sound in 1915, it was moved to the beach road in 1937, where it remains. Today an addition has more than doubled its size.

There was once a modest sign posted in front of St. Andrew's in Nags Head, which urged fishermen to "Come As You Are." My father, Thomas J. Nixon III, captured this message eloquently in the lead-in poem of his second book, *My Pen Is Billed with Brine,* which was published in 1966. "Fishermen" was always my favorite of all his poems.

Fishermen, Come As You Are
Clothed in crusty, rough-hewn,
Weathered cypress shingles
St. Andrews faces outward toward the sea.
Peals from the belfry toll afar
Like those from buoy near the bar,
"Fishermen, come as you are."
Come ye with burdens heavy laden;
Come ye who navigate by star,
Ye who would veer from rocks and shoals,
Or who have fallen short of goals—
Ye who fear to cross the bar.
Come drunkard, harlot, virtuous maiden;
Come all ye, come now to me—
All ye with burdens heavy laden,
Come in to me, ye of the sea;
My nets are strong. I fish for thee.
Yea, fishers come from near and far!
Like fishermen of Galilee,
Who came to you, now come to me.
My garment's weathered; yours may be.
Fishermen, come; come as you are.

OLD MR. HOLLOWELL'S BUSINESS EMPORIUM[2]

When my father spent his childhood summers at Nags Head, there wasn't much there but sand and water and mosquitoes, and the family went by boat where they were met by a horse and cart on the sound side just next to Mr. Hollowell's pier. Although there were no roads then, they did have "double-wides" because the cart wheel rims were twice the normal size, designed to drive in sand.

There was no indoor plumbing or electricity either, nor were there any real grocery stores, drug stores, or hardware stores to speak of, but there was "old Mr. Hollowell's Emporium over on the sound side, which sold a little bit of everything except what you needed," according to my source.[3]

I recalled parts of this story from hearing it in my childhood, but my father's letter clearly illustrated that old Mr. Hollowell was the ultimate entrepreneur, the one with a handle on the pulse of the beach in those days, "the renaissance man of the Outer Banks."

The emporium was later moved to the Beach Road, but the original sound side store had multiple amenities, including a 900-foot pier, which was required to collect any daily mail coming in during low tide, plus ice, "stale bread, and the leather part of a beef roast or so." This was not your ordinary pier, but it was highly functional, complete with narrow gauge steel tracks and a flatbed truck to take mail and stale bread from ship to shore as well as the passengers' freight for the summer.

Since the mail was transported via his pier, it was only natural that our renaissance man was the official postmaster for the area. The daily ritual for the kids, back before 7–11s and malls, was to walk the mile to the post office through hot sand, or deepwater in the flats if it had rained, to meet the boat, "see all of your friends you might have missed on the beach that day," and hang around waiting endlessly for Mr. Hollowell to sort the mail. The kids sent to pick up the mail decided he was a slow reader, until they figured it out. If there were post cards involved, he read every one quickly and might discuss the contents if they were of mutual interest. My father concluded,

"In the absence of newspapers and magazines, he was the best informed native around."

Old Mr. Hollowell was also the "dairyman" for the area, which translates: he found glass bottles on the beach. This wasn't unusual in those days because everyone found glass bottles on the beach then, but Mr. Hollowell found the most and bottled milk in them. Prohibition was in its heyday, but apparently the cruise ships just off the coast managed to get around the Eighteenth Amendment, and they tossed empty bottles overboard, no doubt to destroy the evidence. Old Mr. Hollowell made sure they got recycled about as soon as they hit the beach. My father reported the milk bottles always "rinsed sparkling clean, even though some had a sand-etched opaqueness after being on the bottom for so long." It was only much later that my father learned the difference between a quart and a fifth.

These bottles obviously had to have stoppers to keep the flies out and the contents in, and Mr. Hollowell took care of that end too because the emporium sold fishing supplies, so he naturally sold corks for floats. According to my dad, the corks were always "clean and new, and once you learned the number of the right size float, you had your stopper problem solved."

After our renaissance man milked the cows he kept and corked the contents, the product was ready to go to market. Admittedly, he didn't sanitize by today's standards, and as far as I know, the milk was never pasteurized or homogenized, but none of his customers ever died from it or even got sick, and I expect the "regulars" there built up one heck of an immunity as a result of that dairy business.

Communication was difficult between the Outer Banks and the mainland in those days, but there was a personal touch provided that MCI, AT&T, and Sprint need to know about. If you had a family crisis and had to get word back to the mainland in a hurry, you turned to the Coast Guard. Two patrolmen walked the beach each way, one from the Nags Head station and the other from the Kill Devil Hills station, and once they met in the middle, they would return to their posts. If you had a problem and could find them on your stretch of the beach, they were very conscientious about rushing back to the Coast Guard station to telegraph your message to the station in Elizabeth City, which would then telephone your message to the proper recipient. My father wondered if they called collect. After hearing about this, I wondered why I'd never seen an emergency support system "reach out and touch someone" the way those people did.

As it turns out, there was also a "Mrs. Hollowell," and the two lived next to the store, no doubt to keep a close eye on the business. It was only later I learned they ran a hotel there too, presumably for those who preferred to summer on the sound side, or maybe it was just a hopping off point for those who used the pier. In any event, old Mr. Hollowell now had a hotel, a post office, a dairy business, and a general merchandise store. It was "very general, dealing in dry goods most of the time" per my father, who seemed to recall, "I think he kept some chickens too." If that was the case, I can only assume he had an egg business going as well during his hectic summer season. If that isn't absolute resourcefulness during lean times in a harsh environment, I can't imagine what is.

But my favorite part is when, at age eighty-something, Mr. Hollowell climbed a ladder to his roof in the *middle of a hurricane* to replace a shingle, which had blown away. He did this in spite of "the pleas and importuning of the wind whipped and rain-drenched friends below," and he didn't stop until the task was completed and the descent finished.

Was he more foolhardy than courageous? I don't know. What I do know is he took care of his home, which was obviously his castle, as well as the business emporium, as well as the regulars there, in his own way.

HOT LOVE DURING THE COLD WAR

Now that I think about it, that relationship was hardly "hot." *Platonic* would be a better word, but I think this is a really nifty title and I'd be willing to bet it caught *your* attention! Actually, "Unrequited Love" would be more appropriate, but that's been so overdone nobody wants to read about it anymore, and besides, I thought it would be fun to do a sure-fire titillating title just for the heck of it, but the true story isn't bad.

My dad was a schoolteacher with the summers off, so we spent six weeks at the cottage that year. I was fifteen and *not* looking forward to it because the "in" summer spot for my crowd at home was More-head and sometimes Carolina Beach, but never Nags Head. And here my parents were dragging me off to Nags Head for six entire weeks of my incredibly valuable summer.

I remember the night before we left. My younger brother and I had finished our requirements in preparation for the trip. After dinner Tommy and I sat on the brick wall at the edge of the terrace at dusk and ate the better part of a watermelon. We had a marathon seed-spitting contest into the grass, and that evening I spat hard and fast and my seeds outdistanced his every time. For the first time, I outspat him consistently, which proves that is a handy way to "vent," since people weren't into meditation to relieve stress in those days, especially in Wilson County, North Carolina. All the while we had this seed-spitting contest going on, our parents were packing furiously because they liked to "ride early," in Mama's words.

So we rode early, and we got there and unpacked. Ho hum. And the neighbors were all the same, the beach was the same, and the same stupid waves rolled in the same way they had the last time I was there, and everything considered, fifteen is not a particularly pleasant age for anyone involved, even the fifteen-year-old.

So I got back at my parents by sleeping after I finished my required chores. I slept every chance I could just to illustrate how truly miserable they had made me. I slept just to *show them* how rotten my life was, thanks to them! In retrospect, this nonviolent retribution system could have merit. For example, it could possibly prevent wars, even spousal abuse. Do you recall the movie with Julia Roberts, *Sleeping with the Enemy?* Suppose every time her husband had gone in to beat her up, she had been asleep? Suppose instead she had starred in *Sleeping against the Enemy?*

I don't know if that would have worked for Julia or not. What I do know is, at age fifteen, you can only hold out so long when everyone around you is obviously having so much fun. After about four days of this sleeping binge, I woke up, went out to the beach, and discovered my father in deep conversation with the father of the new family on the block. The family had purchased one of the old Nags Head hotels, and my father obviously had a great rapport with this stranger I had never seen, who looked exactly like Gregory Peck, only more so. Now I'm here to tell you, even a recently awakened fifteen-year-old recognizes "star quality" because it normally doesn't just wash up on the beach, and even if it did, it normally would not be having a deep discussion with your own father.

That night over dinner I told Dad, "Your friend looks exactly like Gregory Peck." He responded, "Who is Gregory Peck?" Parents are absolutely hopeless when you are fifteen, but as Mark Twain observed, they improve with age—your own. Over dinner I asked my father about his new friend and learned he had four children. The eldest, a son who was a year older than I, had recently returned from boarding school in Switzerland.

When I met the younger version of Gregory Peck, my summer changed irrevocably. His eyes and hair were dark, he was intensely serious and initially quite shy, and he made every boy I'd ever met look like homemade soap. I also noticed he had absolutely fantastic male legs in his bathing suit, and I had never noticed male legs in my entire existence, but this guy truly had great legs.

I might as well have been a conch shell that washed up on the beach for all his recognition of me as a female sort of person about his age. I concluded he had been in the Alps too long, so I decided to expose this fellow to some primetime beach heat as I perceived it at age fifteen, which wasn't much. Once I sized up the situation, it became obvious to me that I had to attack on the cerebral level first: I ran all the way home, burst in on my parents and panted, "Okay. You've got to give me some big words, some really great major words to, you know, work into a conversation."

Parents are so weird when you are fifteen. They wanted to know why I had suddenly developed this intense interest in improving my vocabulary to the point it left me out of breath. I finally had to come clean, and once I explained it was the son of Dad's new friend, they gave me *iconoclast* and *esoteric*.

Now I ask you, do you have any idea how hard it is to work *iconoclast*, "breakers of religious icons" into your standard sort of conversation? *Esoteric,* "intended for or understood by only a chosen few; abstruse," was a little easier to squeeze in, but not much. Where *were* my parents coming from?

I was almost always at the hotel after my duties

at the cottage were finished. It was a wonderful place to be, and everything was right there at your fingertips. The food was great, and I got to know everyone on the staff. The original Gregory Peck, my father's friend, knew exactly why I was there and seemed to get a chuckle out of it. Didn't take him long to figure that out! And I got to know the college students who worked there as waitresses for the summer, and they were really nice to me, which was very flattering at age fifteen because they were older and in college. They would frequently have me up to their rooms when they weren't working, which was fun, and they were most encouraging about my "campaign." I came to love that old hotel.

Once the younger Gregory Peck finished his duties around the hotel, he actually started inviting me out to the beach with him. We frequently sat on the sand together in front of the hotel to talk and watch the breakers roll in. Those waves that had seemed stupid only a short time before had improved dramatically. It was amazing.

And I worked in *iconoclast* and *esoteric,* believe it or not, but I recall I had to alter the general theme of the conversation considerably to do it, so it probably wasn't worth the effort in the end. *He,* of course, knew the words. That's okay. I've known them ever since. Besides, he was a year older and had had more exposure.

Ironically, the one topic I introduced that had a lasting impact was totally unplanned. During one of our talking/wave-watching sessions, I told him about something that was a genuine concern to me. It definitely caught his attention. He had been living in Switzerland, a neutral country, and consequently had less exposure to the not-so-Cold War with Russia. Most of my friends were as frightened by it as I, and this became evident when we allowed ourselves to discuss it. After all, half the adults in the nation were building bomb shelters right and left in anticipation of a possible nuclear holocaust. Those were scary times. That definitely caught his attention. He initially got quite pensive, and then he wanted to discuss it at length, which we did. Shortly after that he started digging a bomb shelter under the hotel. As my waitress friends told me, they heard only two sounds when they went to bed at night, the breakers crashing and his digging through the sand. One of my older friends said, "You don't suppose he's undermining the foundation of the hotel do you?" I wasn't sure.

Our relationship "developed," which translates: we became close buddies. He had a motor scooter, and when he wasn't working at the hotel or digging, we took off on his scooter to explore. We discovered the Nags Head woods the way they were then and tromped around in the old graveyard there, brushing off headstones in search of the oldest one. We were careful not to step on the graves. We covered a lot of ground and a lot of history on that motor scooter, and it was a wonderful time of discovery in a beautiful place. We found friends our age within walking distance, and our crowd became established. This was rapidly becoming the most stupendous summer of my life, and by then, I would have defied anyone who tried to drag me to Morehead or Carolina Beach!

One late afternoon when he and I were sitting on the wide deck across from the cabana, which was part of the hotel, a member of our crowd showed up. She was a neighbor, and I liked everything about her except (a) her absolutely incredible physical attributes, plus (b) the fact that she had a minimum of 278 bathing suits, while I had three.

I am here to tell you a fact of life. Even at age fifteen, women have a sixth sense about where other women are coming from, which became quite obvious when she bounced across the deck in her latest hot bikini and "modeled" it for him. It didn't take a sixth sense to figure this one out, and I suddenly yearned to be in Morehead, Carolina Beach, anywhere but there. She did a regular dog and pony show in that bikini and ended with, "What do you think?" He responded, "I think your legs need to fill out." She wasn't a problem after that.

The crowd gave me an unforgettable going-away party my last night on the beach. They brought food, and this became a moveable feast in the finest sense of the word as we splashed up the beach at the edge of the surf. From time to time we would take a break, move to higher ground, graze on the goodies they brought, and then move on. He and I took a brief swim together, and the moonlight illuminated our journey and transformed the phosphorus in the waves to millions of elusive diamonds. When we tried to catch one, it always escaped our grasp, no matter how quick we were.

A stranger, who was obviously drunk, wandered onto the beach and discovered us. When he first tried to join us, we did our best to be kind. When this stranger focused his attention on me, my "love" knocked him out cold in the surf. The drunk's behavior was totally abrasive, but this resolution surprised me. We pulled the poor fellow to high ground well beyond high tide's reach and continued our movable feast.

The next morning my family planned to "ride early," so I ran to the hotel having no idea where I'd find him so early in the morning, but I had to say good-bye. I found him digging. I suspect in this instance he may have been out early after the long night before in an attempt to put the one ugly incident from the previous night behind him, but I can't be sure.

I told him good-bye. He wiped off his hand, took my hand, and gave me the warmest handshake I have ever gotten. It was then he said something memorable, and I remember it was memorable, but for the life of me I can't recall it, no matter how I try. I had really hoped for a kiss.

Not long after that his family sold the hotel and moved away. Years later I heard he had graduated from Harvard which translates, he no doubt drives a Mercedes or BMW now rather than a motor scooter. And I would be willing to bet any number of women have told him what great legs he has, but I never did.

When we got home that summer we discovered a long watermelon vine which ran all the way from the terrace to the driveway. Best of all, it had produced perfect watermelons. Tommy and I must have done quite a job with our seed-spitting contest. Normally I would have gotten excited about this, but after my recent time at Nags Head, seed-spitting contests and being combative with my younger brother didn't seem so important anymore.

BEWARE OF
THE BAYBERRY
BUSHES

If you've visited the Outer Banks, I expect you have
selected that destination based on the recommenda-
tion of friends who have been there, or you may have
gone online in search of a great vacation spot for the
family or a group of friends. It was my experience
that this was normally a family choice, but it could
well have been a group choice if it was planned for
favorite friends who wanted to get away from work,
enjoy the warmth of the beaches with comfortable
friends, and simply relax.

The next step in that pursuit of fun in the sun was
to call the multitude of real estate companies there
and order their brochures so you, or your group, could

personally pick your perfect getaway, and it was usually a toll-free call which made this system very user friendly. So, with thoughts of summer, everybody ordered by calling the toll-free numbers, or went to the companies' Web sites to order a glossy brochure of all the possibilities that particular company had to offer. The possibilities and selections were overwhelming once all those brochures started loading up the mailbox. The decision was usually based on cost, number of people in the party, and what time of year they planned to go, because off-season rates are less, and even those vary depending on time of year.

And the pictures in the brochure don't lie. Either it *is* or not. Those photographs run the gamut from the "glitz" as I call the "mini-hotels," with every amenity, even three elevators in some cases, to the most humble abode. It is enough to make you wonder what happened to Old Nags Head and the original reason for going there.

In any event, the pictures don't lie—even when taken from the best angle—but sometimes the copy that follows below the picture departs from the truth just a tad. I know this because, for reasons passing understanding, I volunteered to edit and write descriptive copy for a number of our properties when I worked for a real estate company there. Since I'd done inspections and inventories on many of the properties, I was quite familiar with most of those I described. I started with the number of bedrooms, baths, and half-baths, and stated the occupancy allowed. Of course I wrote glowing statements about all the amenities included, and this was an easy task with the glitzy mini-hotels because they were packed with amenities to the point I was tempted to write, "How many elevators does one joint need?" but of course I couldn't do that. Then there was the other end of the spectrum where I may have had to visit the property again to find a single amenity, and therein lay the challenge.

If you're possibly a first-time visitor and a novice to the brochure descriptions, here are some helpful tips. Warning: If it begins "nestled among the bayberry bushes," you might want to rethink your decision to lock this one in. If that's the only positive mentioned, it could well be next to a heavily traveled, noisy road, miles from a body of water, and it is more than likely dark and full of spiders. Other hot tips include, be wary of "old world charm." Sometimes "original hard wood floors" could translate, "They may be full of splinters," which doesn't work if you're barefooted, and that is if they are in the place where they were originally installed shortly after the first shipwreck off the coast. They could have shifted over time. "A certain eclectic charm" is really scary, and if the only amenity mentioned is "marble threshold" between the hall and bath, renter beware! "Only minutes from the beach" can have various methods of timing, depending on whether you own a helicopter, so you may want to ask how far it actually is from the ocean or sound when you inquire about it.

General warning: If the property described details more about the weather and surrounding area than the property itself, you might want to inquire about the actual property itself. After all, your family or group will be spending their hard-earned money to go there, so find out what you'll be getting. Example of this variety: "Warm, balmy days and spectacular sunsets welcome you to this memorable retreat, within minutes of fine restaurants and shopping." Excuse me, don't you occasionally have "warm, balmy days and spectacular sunsets," as well as some sort of store and eatery where you already live? Just to be sure you want to spend the "warm balmy nights" in your retreat, ask the reservationist for details about the property before locking it in. Don't blame me; my purpose was to flatter each of our valued owners' properties so they got rented, but sometimes it was a challenge to "shine shinola." And after I'd written enough of these descriptions, I would sometimes get punchy and reach a point where time and space took on a different perspective. To escape the tedium, I would write a description on a totally imaginary property:

Number 6911: "The Love Nest"

Oceanfront: South Nags Head

Heated pool, hot tub, two bidets, satin sheets, plush towels, complimentary champagne and maid service provided

(2)BR (2 1/2)baths

Sleeps up to five (your choice)

You and your main squeeze/s will luxuriate in this dream getaway just feet from the breaking waves. Designed with every whim in mind, your new state-of-the-art romantic paradise features two heart-shaped Jacuzzis, wet bars, plush "acoustically correct" velvet walls, mirrored ceilings, and imported crystal chandeliers in both spacious master suites. Extensively equipped, this made-in-heaven escape for lovers is surrounded by a wraparound deck, complete with sauna and hot tub. The boardwalk leads beyond the heated pool and heart-shaped gazebo to the beach, where lovers search for conch shells or take a moonlit stroll at the surf's edge.

Upper level amenities include: 2 King MBRs, FP, Central A/H, MW, DW, W/D, sauna, hot tub, gazebo, five oversized flat screen TVs, surround sound system throughout, multiple video games, Internet hookup, and an exhaustive library of adult movies.

Downstairs amenities include a well-equipped gym, plus a regulation-size pool table, an extensive collection of current CDs and DVDs, as well as a popcorn machine, soda fountain, and stocked wet bar. An adjacent room houses a paintball machine.

For the sporting crowd, there are five ten-speed bikes with helmets, golf clubs, and tennis rackets, plus his and her hang gliders.

How does one price anything that obscene? I can't imagine.

SAILING BY THE SEAT OF YOUR PANTS

Warning: if you happen to be a seasoned sailor, you will surely be disgusted by this account, so save yourself some heartburn and skip to the next chapter. However, if you are a novice sailor, this chapter is for you.

It all started when I visited a friend on a glorious June afternoon. When I pulled into the driveway, I noticed a sailboat in his front yard which appeared to be about twelve to fourteen feet long. It looked like a pretty good boat to me, but what did I know? My entire sailing resume consisted of two sailing lessons I had in Newport, Rhode Island, that occurred years before, plus a trip on my brother's sailboat because he needed me for "ballast," as he phrased it. I had been called a lot of things, but "ballast," which sounds like a lump of something, was not one of them. I've not yet forgiven my brother for that, but we had great fun on the water, and I remember that major sailing term to this day.

The boat in the yard had recently been purchased by my friend's buddy, who had come over that afternoon for the maiden voyage. This was a previously owned boat, so it was a "maiden voyage" for the new owner and his sidekick only. The boat had been out many times before, and the guys were incredibly enthusiastic about this wonderful sailing adventure.

In all fairness, I will say those two were quite accomplished in a number of areas, but sailing was obviously not one of them. As far as I knew, neither had ever been on a sailboat, much less sailed one. But to their credit, they had already practiced rigging the boat, which seemed like a good idea to me. I didn't want to intrude on their excitement, so I started to leave. My friend stopped me dead in my tracks. "Wait! You can't leave. You've got to teach us how to sail!"

I can't imagine when I'd told that guy I had sailed before, but apparently I had mentioned it because he turned to his friend and said, "She knows how to sail, and she can teach us." I thought that was a pretty scary prospect, as in the blind leading the blind, and I tried to convey how limited my experience was. That fell on deaf ears. I tried to explain that extremely smart people spend entire lifetimes perfecting the science of sailing, and when the journey is done there is still more to learn. That fell on deaf ears. I told them smart people write entire books about the art of sailing. I argued, "For crying out loud, William F. Buckley wrote a book about sailing, and everybody knows he had a brilliant mind and a better vocabulary than Webster, even if I don't agree with his politics." That also fell on deaf ears. Those guys were absolutely convinced they could master this "sport" in an afternoon, which gave me a totally new perspective on the ramifications of the term *macho*.

What the heck? I thought. The day was glorious; the breeze was light with no hint of a storm on the horizon. Mainly, I couldn't wait to get out on the water.

Once they got it off the trailer and into the sound, I got a clue about the way the afternoon would go. James, the new owner, asked my friend, "Did you put the plug in?" Ron replied he had indeed plugged it up so it wouldn't leak, which struck me as a good precautionary measure. Ron pulled us past the seaweed, and they put me at the helm to "teach" them.

The term *luffing* came back because the sail was definitely doing that, being hit on both sides by the wind and going absolutely nowhere. Our object was to get to the channel, so I had to recall it, pull it up from somewhere in my memory.

Once I focused on the sail, I began to *feel* it, the wind direction and the flow of the current. That sail caught the wind, and we actually left a wake in the water as we headed for the channel. It wasn't so different from learning to ride a bicycle, because once you have mastered the rudiments they are imprinted on your inherent responses forever.

The terms began to come back, and I started throwing them up for grabs as they surfaced in my mind: "Those are *battens*," and I explained why they were there. I decided to "come about" and let the guys know ahead of time. James wanted to know if that meant "turn around," and I told him it did indeed. Consequently, James referred to this maneuver as "turn around" for the rest of the afternoon. That led me to observe the two distinctly different personalities I was expected to "coach."

James, the new boat owner, was such a low-key sort one was left wondering if he would register a blood pressure level if he were tested. He was very quiet, so when he made a comment, you tended to listen to it. His comments were almost always hilarious, which he didn't seem to realize, but his audience did. James was also a worrier, and he worried about slamming into crab pots and the channel markers most of the afternoon, until he started worrying about the pager calls he got periodically during his maiden voyage on his new boat.

In case you didn't know this, all three members of that crew had pagers because, believe it or not, there were some extremely high-tech types living right there on the Outer Banks. Some of us, however, left our pagers turned off back at the house because there should be a clearly defined line between work and play. If you don't draw that line, you end up with an osmosis effect between the two.

James's pager did exactly what it was designed to do. It beeped in a big way that afternoon, and the more it beeped the more James worried about getting back and the less he worried about the crab pots and the channel markers. That is when *tacking* took on a whole new meaning.

My other "student" appeared to be picking up the sailing terms as quickly as I threw them out. He seemed to try them on for size before throwing them back when a particular term applied. I sensed this was his way of making them part of his vocabulary, which I appreciated, since my children never responded as readily when I tried to teach them something. It was then I recalled that Ron was an avid chess player, and it has been my experience that real chess players generally have two common traits: they tend to be intensely competitive, and they would prefer to be challenged rather than be given a shortcut, any day of the week. I figured this was the type who would opt for a sailboat over a bass boat to get from one place to another because they appear to have a preference for cerebral energy over mechanical energy. I saw some real potential there.

As we headed for the channel, I kept warning them to "mind the sail." And I pointed out the wake left behind us, which is visible evidence you must be doing something right. Then it occurred to me that steering a small boat is not so different from driving a car because if you aren't at the helm, you're

only along for the ride. I offered the tiller to anyone who would take it, and Ron jumped on it. He
started watching the sail closely, and when we hit the
channel he said, "Hey, I remember red, right, return,"
which didn't do a thing for James, who was getting
another pager call.

When we got to the channel, it took me back to
Newport, the place invented with sailing in mind.
The wind hit us with a double whammy! That little boat picked up a real head of steam, and it was
exhilarating! Ron was getting comfortable with the
tiller, and once he settled into it we decided the boat
needed a name, or at least Ron and I did. James was
not overly excited about this boat-naming business,
but we were not deterred. We talked about the America Cup Race and noble boat names, and we tried to
recall the name of Ted Turner's sailboat, which had a
very noble name, but we couldn't remember it.

Then it hit me, the name for this seaworthy little
craft. It was hardly noble, but it was fun and seemed
to fit. "This is *The Blow and Go*." Ron repeated it,
tried it on for size, and then he lost it, laughing over
the name, and said, "James, that's *it!* You have *got* to
name it *The Blow and Go!* It's perfect!" At that point
James was not particularly interested in naming anything because he *had* to get back.

Consequently, I tried to explain what I could
recall about serious tacking upwind, that zigzag
close-hauled course that is challenging and definitely
not designed for the instant gratification crowd. It
was also the only way to get James back unless we

paddled, which is an extremely lubberly thing to do in a sailboat, and besides, it takes longer.

Getting from point A to point B is a piece of cake in a motorboat, but it can be a challenge in a sailboat. I drew an imaginary straight line with my finger and then illustrated the zigzag pattern of cutting back and forth across the original line and said, "You have to work with the wind to make this happen." I had forgotten about the part where the real fun starts when the wind alternately blows and falls off or changes directions constantly, which it has a way of doing on the Outer Banks. The guys took turns trying to catch the wind.

Meanwhile I started to think about the rudder, which is hinged so the lower half kicks up if it hits the bottom in shallow water. Then it struck me, and I said, "Hold it, stop everything! We've got to pull the rudder up and fix it." The rudder had been tied in the kicked-up position the entire trip, so we had been sailing with *half a rudder,* which is surely a brain-dead way to sail. Once that was corrected, that little boat went into overdrive, and the response was amazing. It was like trading up from a Volkswagen to a Mercedes! Ron, who was at the helm, felt the difference immediately and asked, "Didn't I think of this?" I replied, "No, I did," but I didn't mention the fact that I should have thought of it long before since I was the designated "teacher."

Ron's first attempt to get us to our destination left us dead in the water close to the marsh. The wind definitely was not cooperating, and he concluded he had "zagged" too far. He took us back out and headed in again. That time we landed within inches of the spot where we had hoisted sail, or as James referred to it, "pulled the sail up."

I was feeling pretty good about myself as a "teacher," but it is a bit irritating when one of your "students" does a more credible job than you probably could have done yourself!

The guys got the boat back on solid ground in record time, and James left to take care of his calls. Ron had that treasure perched in his yard again, and I drove home, hoping all the way James would name it the *Blow and Go* because it *was* perfect. It fit.

DOES YOUR GRASS CRY WHEN YOU CUT IT?

One of the truly great aspects of living on the Outer Banks was the concept that maintaining a lawn was optional. You were not required to grow grass in your front yard, or your backyard either for that matter. After all, that is sand country!

I personally thought this was a wonderful idea because (a) you don't have to go out and buy very expensive lawn maintenance equipment, plus (b) you don't have to mess with keeping up the outside when (c) you mainly sleep inside anyway, which (d) frees up your weekends.

This is a stupendous theory, and my place was a prime example. My front "yard" consisted of a very steep driveway surrounded by cypress trees dripping with Spanish moss. My backyard was a natural mix of sand, some oyster shells, and whatever happened to sprout there, all enclosed by those great trees draped in moss. That was one high-quality low-maintenance yard.

Every now and then you would see those who made a major move to the Outer Banks so they could "get free," and the first thing they did once they crossed the bridge and got settled in was buy grass seed and fertilizer. Forget it, folks! A well-manicured lawn is *not* a prerequisite for living there. In fact, we discourage it because if you did that it would make the rest of us look bad, and we never moved there to keep up a lawn in the first place.

If you have a problem with withdrawal from lawn maintenance, you might consider this true account told to me by a trusted friend: One Saturday afternoon some demented misfit with nothing but time on his hands decided to test his houseplants' susceptibility to abuse, so he hooked a lie detector up to his philodendron and shredded some of its leaves. The monitor immediately registered an abrupt change in nerve response, which in plant language means, "You better get your scummy hands off me now, or I'll eat you in your sleep." The plant calmed down considerably when this weirdo left the room. When he returned, the plant reacted violently on the monitor, although it was never touched again. Are you ready for that?

Unfortunately for anyone reading this, the experiment didn't end there. This scientific person clearly had a lot of time to kill, so next thing you know he plopped some English ivy next to the philodendron and slapped a lie detector on that one too. Then he left the room, probably to go to the bathroom, and when he returned to the room, both plants went nuts, although neither plant was touched.

I don't know what you've gotten out of this unbelievably educational story, but I concluded that these plants not only could experience pain, but they could recall it and even chat with each other about it afterward. That's a pretty scary prospect if you choose to dwell on it for much over a minute. As a result, I wouldn't blame the plants a bit if they tried to get us back, and we could all be facing the revenge of the sneaky stamens sometime tomorrow before lunch.

There may be a few houseplants out there who are hurting and not communicating their pain and not revolting, but I suspect they are pretty up-tight and, no doubt, vote Republican.

As I mentioned, a trusted friend told me this so I believe it, although I've discovered it generally doesn't pay to accept something at face value until you've slept on it. I certainly slept on this one and figured it out. This cretin who went around smushing plant leaves obviously didn't have Mrs. Abernathy for biology. I figure this low-life's wife left him about seven weeks before, there was no food in the house and no decent sports on TV, so what else does he have to do on the weekend?

This scenario presents two obvious questions that I wish someone would answer for me:

1. Where did he get the lie detector monitors in the first place?

2. Was that guy smoking oregano or what?

Mrs. Abernathy would have sifted through scientific evidence like this and reached a conclusion, so I figured that was a proper approach. I figured if your withered houseplants hurt that badly when you messed with them, can you imagine how your grass agonizes every week when you cut it? The pain must be insufferable. I'll bet when you lived in the suburbs, every time you opened the garage door to drive to work your grass thought you were bringing out the lawn mower. That would be a horrible way to live, and I want no part of it. I decided shortly after hearing that story that I would never touch a lawnmower again. This philosophy served me well for a number of years, and it played particularly well on the Outer Banks.

If you insist on cutting your grass every weekend, should you choose to grow it in a beach environment, you are in for big trouble, and don't say I didn't warn you. Have you ever heard of killer cucumbers? My research has revealed these seemingly benign cucumbers are first cousins, once removed, from the grass in your front yard. You pull that lawn mower out one more time and the cukes will get you in the end!

WELLNESS TODAY

When you live at the beach, you quickly realize you are going to have to show up in a bathing suit sooner or later if you choose to enjoy the best amenity of all, the ocean, which is the reason many of us assembled there in the first place. Now don't get me wrong. I am all for lean, tan bodies, but that all-consuming exercise syndrome started to get on my nerves. I don't know about you, but I was personally getting sick of low fat, high fiber, and being intimidated by those runners who clogged up the end of my driveway when I was trying to get to work in the morning.

My first question about this wellness kick is, if people like to run so much, why do they have to wear portable music to get through it? Besides, where did they get the leisure to run past my mailbox while I was stuck with driving to work on the bypass? Were those people independently wealthy or simply out of work? And if they were out of work, how could they afford those expensive running shoes that cost more than their mortgage?

There was a time I forced myself to run regularly, but the only "endorphin high" I ever experienced was a tremendous relief every time it was over. As a result, I decided running is dangerous for your health for several reasons. If you run on concrete, it can really mess up your knees, and then you have to go through extremely expensive outpatient surgery, which also costs more than your mortgage even after insurance covers 80 percent of it—that is, if you have insurance in the first place. The really life-threatening aspect of running lies in exploring your neighborhood without a car to protect you. You could have a heart attack, which is preferable to being brought down by a pit bull or Rottweiler, or the neighborhood kids racing for the ice cream truck.

Now that we've covered the running syndrome, what I'd really like to address here is America's obsession with high fiber and low fat. High fiber has been around a while, but as I recall, it seemed the low-fat neurosis kicked in shortly after the troops returned from the Persian Gulf War and CNN was no longer all-consuming. America has been on a low-fat kick ever since, and this has currently evolved to lengthy discussions on trans fat, which is about as exciting as nasal polyps.

For the record, I want you to know that I believed in high fiber to the point I bought a very expensive box of the highest fiber cereal available because I read somewhere you're supposed to do that. I took it home but couldn't bring myself to open it because the picture on the front looked like petrified worms. I don't know what's happened to marketing in this country, but if that box was an indication, I'd say it's gone down the tubes. For starters, there were no pictures of bananas or strawberries on the front, and the back of the box was filled with totally boring nutritional information printed in bland earth colors, which was not worth reading while munching the contents, if I had been crazy enough to do that in the first place. Their idea of a prize inside would probably have been a little brown bag of tofu. I just hope those marketing geniuses never get their hands on Cracker Jacks!

I was especially confounded by the low-fat craze because it seemed to ignore the calories and carbohydrates, which I always thought were the major instigators of yucky bodies in America. For example, I was once eating a rare combination of chocolate pudding, whipped cream, and crushed Oreos, but I felt some guilt about it and said so in front of relatively sane people. I couldn't believe the unanimous response I got. "Don't worry. It's low in fat!" That struck me as about the finest rationalization I've heard since I got old enough to vote, and one I could come to live with very easily. The only problem is, if I build my life around crushed Oreos and whipped cream, I'll end up having to run to get rid of them, and we all know what running can do to your health.

• • •

I had a grandmother who lived to be a hundred years old, more or less, which is pretty amazing considering the fact that she never heard of holistic medicine, much less the current wellness craze or ugly cereal. That tiny woman scarfed down pork chops and eggs, never drank water, and her biggest vice and greatest treat was one scalding hot cup of coffee first thing in the morning. She always walked fast, but she never ran, probably because she was cost conscious and didn't want to pay for the shoes. She also had the good sense to realize the best part of fried chicken is the skin, and I expect if she were alive to hear all this hoopla about high fiber and low fat, she would chuckle and go on about her business.

She had an interesting way of chuckling, which brings to mind one of her best comments. She adored her two great-grandchildren. On our last visit with her some years ago, she encouraged them to tell her about that days adventure of seeing Shamu the whale near Disney World. As each competed to tell the best story, getting louder and more abrasive in the process, she finally chirped in, "Isn't it just a big fish jumping up and down in a puddle?"

I have no idea where a sense of humor comes from; it's probably fried chicken skin, but I suspect longevity comes from good genes. If you happen to be stuck with skimpy genes, you may be able to hedge your bets just around the corner at your local fitness center. I'm talking about body-banging aerobics with members of the opposite sex in front of mirrors and flat screen TVs. I've seen those places, and they normally have great equipment, maybe a sauna, and a "special introductory offer." I think they start with a simple spinal tap to determine your genetic potential so they can design your own individualized exercise program, plus they allow you to run on an inside track so you won't be brought down by neighborhood kids in search of the ice cream truck.

THE BERMUDA TRIANGLE EFFECT

The experts tell us the Bermuda Triangle is more or less defined as a triangular region (no surprise there) in the Atlantic Ocean that stretches from Bermuda to Puerto Rico to Florida. This dark hole is that place in the universe where, ever since the 1940s, both ships and aircraft have reputedly disappeared and abnormal events tend to occur for no apparent reason. This is what the experts tell us.

What do they know? The experts can believe whatever they want to, but anyone on the Outer Banks can tell you that one of those angles is all wrong because the Bermuda Triangle *actually* reaches from Bermuda to Puerto Rico to the Outer Banks of North Carolina; or at least it does during the summer months. That angle definitely moves our way over Memorial

Day and establishes itself. It may move back to Florida after Labor Day, but it is surely there during the summer, which not only explains all the shipwrecks off the coast, but also bizarre vacation behavior.

Everybody loves vacation. After all, you save for it, dream about it, and live it vicariously for about seventeen weeks before you actually experience that one week in the sun, two at best. Little wonder it always seems too short! Hey, everybody goes a little nuts over vacation, and that is only human. We have all been there. However, there are some vacation stories that are so unbelievable they make you wonder what this nation has been doing wrong the other fifty-one weeks of the year.

When you live in an area where tourism drives the economy, you observe a real cross-section of vacation behavior. Thankfully most of it is normal. Every now and then, however, you encounter behavior patterns so bizarre they defy explanation. Consequently, some creative soul dubbed this phenomenon "the Brain Bank" and the name stuck. The Brain Bank is a common local reference to those imaginary brain depositories strategically located at the west end of bridges crossing over to the banks. I figured some of our visitors were so accustomed to paying a toll to cross a bridge that they couldn't adapt when they encountered a bridge without a toll booth, so they automatically dropped their brains there because they have been conditioned to make a deposit of some sort.

I've found the best reporters of this Brain Bank

phenomenon are the cleaners, maintenance people, and police up and down the beach, because they experience it firsthand and tell it like it is. Some of their stories are definitely worth sharing.

One of our great maintenance people reported this one, and when it comes to pure creativity, I would put this near the top of any list. I will preface this by saying that I am all for eating fresh seafood, and steaming seafood not only brings out the flavor, but it is better for the cholesterol level than frying. However, I draw the line at steaming seafood in the dishwasher! I found this dishwasher-steaming concept to be so innovative that I told my brother about it. Once he stopped laughing, he asked if they put Old Bay seasoning in the little soap dispenser cup. Since my brother is a good cook, he would naturally think of major cooking tips like this.

When I worked in property management, I met a delightful rookie with one of our police departments during the course of an eviction, and he appeared to be suffering from shellshock. Actually, he was not technically a rookie, because he had served as a policeman for eight years on the mainland before moving to the Outer Banks. Unfortunately, he was finding a bit more action on our coast than he had bargained for, but only because his timing was a bit off. He had moved to the Outer Banks shortly before Beach Week kicked in, so it was not surprising that he was suffering from shell shock. Hopefully he remained long enough to realize it calms down considerably afterward, because he struck me as a very nice person who would be a real asset.

The Outer Banks is definitely a family beach, and this is generally a family sort of book, but some of the upcoming stories have been rated PG-13. These are included because no inside scoop on the Outer Banks would be complete without them. Once you get wind of hot stuff like this, you realize you're sitting on something with all the dramatic elements, of say, the O.J. trial, only this is better because those maintenance people and cleaners never mess with "going to sidebar." They simply tell the story.

I went to "the source" for these juicy tidbits, and my ultimate source was one of the finest cleaners on the beach. Jessie, of Jessie's Cleaning Service, ran a a corporation on wheels. When it heated up during peak season, she had up to twenty-five crews cleaning rental properties from Corolla to South Nags Head during that five- to six-hour window between check-out and check-in. This woman and her crews had their fingers on the pulse of vacation behavior, since they were the ones who encountered the treasures left behind from the previous week.

I don't know about you, but if I walked into a cottage and found "ten to twelve empty family size Cool Whip containers surrounding the Jacuzzi," I'd wonder where the strawberries were. On second thought, this incident probably had nothing to do with strawberries, but being the good investigative reporter I am, I asked if there were any whipped cream squirt cans present on the premises. The answer was no, so

I concluded that crowd was not as innovative as they might have been. But what do I know?

We rented primarily to family groups, and per my source, this was obviously a family group, a very large family reunion spread over four adjacent cottages in South Nags Head. That one definitely got the vote when it came to feeding a big crowd in a hurry. I'm talking major innovation here, the sort fast food chains need to know about.

When Jessie arrived to clean something at their request, she found lettuce wedges, whole cucumbers, and carrots being rinsed in the washing machine. The food preparation crew was waiting for the spin cycle to dry them. Meanwhile they had found one of those zippered pillow covers and stuffed it to the gills with hot dog and hamburger rolls, zipped it closed, and had the rolls tossing in the dryer to warm. Now that's the sort of meal you hate to miss!

This brings to mind a question I was asked several times. When a potential visitor saw "outside shower" advertised in our brochure, he occasionally asked if there was indoor plumbing. Actually that was a logical question if you hadn't been there before because that place was definitely remote compared to the norm. That, after all, was the beauty of it. Consequently, I explained the outside showers existed to wash off beach sand before entering the property, and I tried to reassure our first-time visitors that we did indeed have indoor plumbing as well as multiple television options, VHS, DVD players, and fax and ATM services, plus many cottages have all the wiring and high-tech widgets to run your business from there if you didn't pack your laptop. You could certainly do that on your vacation, which seems counterproductive to me, but if that's what you want, knock yourself out. In other words, the Outer Banks has all the comforts of home without the headaches. But I didn't realize until I talked with my source that we also had multiple purpose household appliances, which not only wash and dry clothes and dishes, but also steam seafood, wash and spin-dry vegetables, as well as warm hamburger rolls. All things considered, I think those Kenmores, Whirlpools, etc. should cost more because if that isn't multitasking, I don't know what is. (I couldn't bring myself to ask what that crowd did with the blender.)

The ultimate appliances were hot tubs and Jacuzzis, which were much in demand. The hot tubs were cleaned and maintained on a weekly basis by the companies that installed them, and the Jacuzzis were taken care of by the cleaning crews. Jessie and Co. had cleaned more Jacuzzis than you could count in a lifetime, but this one stood out in her mind. When she entered a particular bathroom, she discovered the Jacuzzi half full of congealed red Jell-O, which had obviously been stirred up a bit. Now I ask you, how many boxes of Jell-O would it take to gel that volume at room temperature? I had no idea, but this led me to imagine the grocery order for a quick run to Food Lion: "Honey, could you pick up bread, milk, and 190 boxes of Jell-O?" In this instance, "Honey" picked up red Jell-O, but my source could not confirm whether it was cherry or strawberry because she decided not to taste it.

We got a perplexing hot tub call once. Our caller wanted to know if we had any cottages in the Corolla area with a "hot tub in the kitchen." We didn't, but I thought that was a novel concept since hot tubs were normally on outside decks. I'll leave this for you to figure out, but I personally wondered if that guy was recalling those Saturday night baths of yesteryear when they dragged the tub to the kitchen and heated the water over a wood stove.

After doing a number of cleaning inspections there, I discovered three areas that tend to separate the sheep from the goats when it comes to cleaners. The good cleaners actually dust the backs of TV sets as well as the fronts and tops. They thoroughly clean the base and backs of toilets in addition to the business part, and they never miss the inside top of the microwave. Since my source and her crews did it right, you can imagine their surprise when they opened a microwave and discovered two pairs of bikini panties inside. One can only speculate about the reason they were there and my source wondered if they were drying them, warming them up, or simply trying to take care of a yeast infection. Your guess is as good as mine, but in this instance those items were not mailed back to the owner.

We referred to prime time summer arrival days as "show time" because there is a world of activity going on behind the scenes during that window between check-out and check-in. As soon as a visitor checked out, an inventory was done, and then the cleaners took over. After they finished, a cleaning inspector followed with a check-off list and a cleaner or crew would be called back to correct anything overlooked before the next guest ever saw the property.

As our visitors arrived in full force on the bypass, the stage was being set all around them. This involved thousands of cottages and hundreds of people who went into overdrive to do what it took to keep our guests coming back. The cleaning crews went into high gear to pull that together in a brief time span, so when my source got a beeper call from one of her old reliable crews and was told, "You've got to get over here right now," she responded immediately. When she arrived she found the freezer door open and one of her cleaners, an older man, doubled over in laughter. The freezer was packed to capacity with frozen condom "missiles." True story again.

My source speculated the creators had hooked the top edge of these devices over cardboard paper towel tubes, filled them with water, tied the tops and left them to freeze. Once the "missiles" froze, the tube was removed. That freezer was packed to the gills with those things. Jessie gave this some thought and said, "Or they might have used PVC pipe and run them under hot water to remove them from the mold."

I don't know about you, but this situation raised a few questions in my mind. What did they plan to *do* with them? Then I wondered if their vacation week had been spoiled by rain, and if so, couldn't they find something better to do, for crying out loud? Did they save up all year for that great vacation in order to go there and make condom missiles? Do they not have a freezer at home? After that expenditure of energy, why did they leave their treasures behind? The Outer Banks sells lots of cheap coolers, and ice is readily available. Were they planning to play war games? Whatever the motive, that crowd turned "show time" into *primetime* for one cleaning crew on that beach one hectic summer Saturday.

According to my source, creativity takes many forms, and this one landed rather close to home. When Jessie showed up to clean a cottage that was expected to be vacant, she was greeted at the door by the owner's grandson and his girlfriend. The grandson was decked out in the girlfriend's underwear and negligee while the girlfriend was more or less clad in a fishnet thing that left little to the imagination. Consequently, my source called the grandmother and cleaned the cottage the following day after the grandson was told to leave. I certainly appreciated the delicacy of that situation that involved a cottage owner. At the same time, I couldn't help but appreciate the fishnet outfit, which is a nice nautical touch that meshes well on barrier islands.

After getting this earful, I concluded the "experts" could believe whatever they chose about the placement of that third angle of the Bermuda Triangle. Meanwhile, I am absolutely convinced that particular angle crawls up the coast from Florida to the Outer Banks between Memorial Day and Labor Day. After all, the *real* experts live there, and believe me, *they have proof!*

THE LONG AND WINDING ROAD

The four-mile stretch full of twists and turns on the way back to Colington Harbour offers a real cross-section of life. I doubt you would find that road mentioned in any of the guidebooks, but I think it is worth noting because every now and then, around a bend, there is a glimpse of life the way it used to be on the banks.

Once you make the turn west at the gas station/convenience store on the bypass, the road starts out dead serious, but don't be fooled by that. It loosens up considerably a curve or two away, where the drive is punctuated by the sound and inlets and crab pots and the people who make their living from the sea. After a long day, the drive home around the twists and turns could sometimes be frustrating, but all in all, it beat commuting on the expressway every time.

It is one twenty-first-century road at the beginning. There are more goods and services in the first three-block radius than you can shake a stick at. Not only do you find the municipal center and the Veterans' Memorial, plus the chamber of commerce, the post office, and library, but there is also the senior citizens' center, the board of realtors, and a CPA firm. The area is chock full of faxing, computer, secretarial, and mailing services, plus a rent-all place if you need a food warmer or tent in a hurry. There is also a "reverse osmosis" plant, and I haven't figured out precisely what that is, but it sounds quite complex. I haven't spotted a law firm in that section, but there may be one located just down the road at the trash disposal place. I haven't personally checked this out.

The good news is, once you get past the first block or so, there is a thick stand of pines bordering the asphalt on both sides and a small airstrip just to your right as you drive west. On a good day, you may spot a small plane revving its engines preparing for takeoff, or a biplane could fly low overhead leveling its wings on final approach for landing adjacent to the Wright Memorial. It seems appropriate in "the Land Where Flight Began."

As you continue to drive west, you will find the Colington Café to your left, nestled under cypress trees in a romantic setting. Reservations are required, but it is worth the effort to plan ahead in that instance. I put the Colington Café right up there with Owens' Restaurant, which has been doing it right on the Outer Banks since 1946. Even Andy Griffith will tell you about Owens', but I suggest you find out for yourself.

At one time there was a new kid on the block just beyond the Colington Café on the same side of the road. That place fascinated me because the marquis once advertised "Exotic Dancers." Not long after that, it stated: "Closed. Gone fishing." That announcement remained for several months, which led me to ponder several questions:

1. Where did the exotic dancers go? Did they go fishing too?

2. Did the person who said he went fishing really go fishing, or did he follow the exotic dancers?

3. If he followed the dancers and was married at the time, how did his wife feel about that?

4. Why is it every time you need decent help on the Outer Banks, half the work force has gone fishing?

Not far away you will find Joe and Kay's Campground, which is a major trailer park. Just in case you miss the entrance, there is a large sign to help you out with an arrow pointing left as you drive west. The large letters advise you to turn left, but if you mess up and turn right anyway, you will end up in the dirt parking lot of the Blue Crab Tavern, which sits on the water. When it comes to pure "picturesque," that place has it. There are beer signs and usually some T-shirts hanging in the front window. This is a watering hole of a bygone era, except for the beer signs, which are neon, a clear indication of progressive thinking. The Blue Crab was a natural for the guys who built the bridges nearby, as well as a number of locals and natives at the end of a long day. The only problem with sipping suds on the barstools there too long is you could suffer an untimely death, in which case you could land down the road at Hilltop Cemetery, which is appropriately named because it is the only high ground in a low-lying area. I decided that would be an ideal place to bury a loved one because there are great sound views, and mainly, you would never have to worry about seepage. I don't know if there are any slots left or even if there is a waiting list, but if there is an overwhelming demand, maybe they should consider going condo. You know—stack 'em.

After making that drive a time or two, I realized you could live almost anywhere along that stretch and never have to leave in a lifetime except to show up for work. It is all right there at your fingertips. At that time there was a dentist, an auto and marine clinic, a pet grooming shop, even a pawn shop where you could get "Cash in a Flash" if you were down on your luck. I didn't spot a doctor's office, but that might not present a problem if you eat lots of fish, grow your own vegetables, and don't hang out at the Blue Crab too long. Seafood companies dot this road at almost every turn, but there are two which fascinated me. On the drive back you may spot a typical Outer Banks fishing boat sitting on the front lawn of a home just beyond Joe and Kay's Campground. "Fresh Crabs and Shrimp" is painted on its side, which is a great marketing technique, but the most memorable aspect of that boat showed up one Christmas when its outline was etched in tiny white lights, while the bottom was highlighted in blue lights, like the sea. That was an unforgettable sight on a cold winter night.

The second seafood place that riveted my attention is Endurance Seafood. With a name like that, how could they go wrong? I wondered if those Endurance people had a special handle on prolonging the life of regular seafood. Did that crowd "flash freeze" or what? (Inquiring minds *definitely* want to know information like that.)

I think it was Ben Franklin who said something about fish and guests stinking after three days, but as far as fish are concerned, I decided Ben didn't know about Endurance Seafood. Ben was also wrong about guests, but I can't blame him for that because he spent a good part of his life in Philadelphia, which didn't have a beach the last time I checked. He had no way of knowing this: When you live at the beach, people you never heard of in your life will come to visit you. People you shared a taxi with in a strange city will come to visit you if you live at the beach, and they are the ones who always bring their brother-in-law. So Ben missed the boat on that one because some guests stink after about three *hours;* but all in all, Ben

Franklin was a great statesman and diplomat. More importantly, he conducted highly scientific experiments with kites, which culminated in Kitty Hawk Kites, located directly across the bypass from Jockey's Ridge.

Years ago when the guys completed the second bridge on the way to Colington Harbour, they did a great job. I got to know the faces after driving past them so often, so there was almost a vicarious pleasure in their job well done. That is one high-tech bridge, complete with nifty little reflector lights along both sides to keep you from slamming into it at night should you be inclined to do that. Thankfully, the newly improved bridge still allows you to get to one of the finest crabbing spots on the Outer Banks, which used to be next to the old bridge. Families are there constantly, and the children love it best. There is something instantly gratifying about throwing out a chicken neck attached to a string and pulling up something exciting. Better yet, you can take your catch home to steam, spread some newspapers, and eat your heart out. That is down-home messy eating at its best, and the kids especially love it because the most rewarding part of all is, they caught their own dinner.

When it was referred to as "the new road" leading to Colington Harbour, I gave those infrastructural experts who designed it my bottom line. The original road builders were pretty smart when they saved the best for last. That is where the road makes an almost-180 degree turn to accommodate the

Colington United Methodist Church, a lovely little clapboard church that sits across the road from the sound. "You infrastructural people mess with that curve and *you are yesterday's road kill!* It's okay if you repave it. You could fill in some potholes since you're going to be in the area anyway, and feel free to dot and dash it with your yellow paint, but if you change the curve around that church, don't say I didn't warn you!"

Once you reach Colington Harbour, you will find a mixed bag in terms of real estate, which runs the gamut from the simple to the stately, but the best real estate of all sits on the water and is either sail or motor driven. I've found when you sidestep the obvious you sometimes find the unusual. I discovered that in the side yard of a waterfront home in the harbor. A larger than life "watermelon" is actually a gas tank. Apparently some free spirit saw this and painted that delightful bit of whimsy, which sheds a whole new light on the old adage, "When life gives you a lemon, make a watermelon."

There was something reinforcing about living at the end of a road like that, but even there it was easy to fall prey to the same constraints that dominated my life back on the mainland. For example, when I was running late for work, it was tempting to navigate the curves at warp speed, until I happened upon a crabber or fisherman who was also driving to work—on the water next to me. That's when I got my reality check for the day and recalled my original reason for "coming home."

"LOCUST" 1-2-3[4]

The vacation rental business on the Outer Banks, and everywhere else in the civilized world, is generally computer driven, as are most businesses. There is no way anyone could keep track of all the weeks rented for so many homes, much less handle the property managing aspects of that business without computers. This doesn't mean I have to *like* computers, and I thought Bill Gates looked a bit suspicious at first, but I have gotten more comfortable with them. There was a time computers left me with the queasy feeling Dan Quayle would probably have gotten if he had been the featured speaker at a Mensa convention.

I was inherently *not* a child of the twentieth century, and most assuredly not the twenty-first, but I will admit the twentieth century had its good points, and the twenty-first seems to be coming along fairly well, thank you very much. After all, the twentieth century produced penicillin, the birth control pill, and dishwashers, so as centuries go, it wasn't all bad. But the most innovative twentieth-century invention, which stands heads and shoulders above the rest, is the thermos bottle. "Why?" you might ask. Reasonable question. The answer is, "It keeps hot things hot and cold things cold." Should you question why that is such a nifty concept, I would ask you, "How does it know?"

The thermos was so cleverly crafted, it inherently knows what to do. Computers don't, and they're only as good as the directions you give them. Although they may be useful for managing rental property, they can't do dip when it comes to keeping your soup hot or your iced tea cold, so how great are they in the overall scheme of things?

Since I basically didn't trust computers in the twentieth century, I find it amazing, in retrospect, that I ended up with two husbands who thought computers were the best thing since butter beans. I remember when my first husband got a computer, and that was years ago. I recall it because we gave up major grocery money so he could buy this incredibly high-tech twentieth-century device. He spent endless hours toying with it, and I'll never forget the loudest yell he ever yelled, and he was a first-rate yeller. He'd been punching in all sorts of vital information one night and forgot to save it. It was gone forever out there in the cyber galaxy. This led me to wonder why the damn thing didn't have a "flush" button on it in the first place since it seemed to like losing information shortly after it was entered. Face it: The computer wants you to go away because it prefers to sit and hum, quietly displaying its Saver Screen, and the last thing it wants is for someone to go pecking around on its keys and giving it orders. What I can't understand is why the bloody thing doesn't have a "go away" button, or better yet, an "I have a headache" button, although now that I think about it, it would be difficult to cram "I have a headache" all on one button. Maybe they could spread it over two buttons and place them on opposite corners of the keyboard while requiring you to hit the shift key simultaneously. That would really drive people nuts.

It wasn't long after he forgot to save, that my ex-husband joined a computer group. They got together several nights a week after work and talked over their problems, the way I suppose AA does, and next thing you know he was establishing one-on-one communication with his "system." He transferred it to his office and back home again with all the information right where it was supposed to be, according to him. It was as if the computer had sprouted wings.

I had a way of treading directly from the frying pan into the fire when it came to computers. My second husband cut his teeth on dot matrix eons ago, and if you ever had a desire to see major twentieth-century sophistication at its finest, you definitely would have identified with our "computer room." The dot matrix was primarily for spreadsheets on his job. The laser printer was for serious stuff or any-one you needed to really impress. (And all the while, I'd thought lasers were for logos on credit cards and knee surgery.) The copier was great for children's homework assignments, newspaper clips, and recipes worth repeating, but the most serious gadget of all was a futuristic label maker that spun around with a multitude of lights and sounds, just like a political convention. After it did a regular dog and pony show, it actually spat out labels, which was precisely what it was designed to do, but it didn't have balloons or ticker tape like a convention, so I wasn't particularly impressed.

The end result was, we had all that high-tech equipment in our home, and all it did was *sit* there humming with all its attachments and wires and life support systems, which occupied so much space that we came to refer to this highly evolved hodgepodge as "the computer room." Now I ask you, have you ever commanded that sort of attention in a lifetime? When was the last time you had an *entire* room named after you, especially one with a mortgage?

I personally never had a room named for me, particularly one with a mortgage, but my grandfather did name his boat after me. My name was painted on a sign that was always attached to the boat when I visited. At age eight I knew I was about the best thing on the block when we went out on the lake in "my" boat. It wasn't a particularly big boat, not nearly as big as the room the computer and life support systems occupied, but it could float. I wondered if that computer could have floated. I rather doubt it, but I'd have loved to try it.

Resistance to computers is a clear indicator of age, and I've found the following to be absolute computer truths of life:

1. Generally, if you're a computer owner over sixty, maybe fifty years old, you may be in over your head already. Either accept that, or get help from the six-year-old kid next door. Bribes work well in this situation.

2. Conversing with friends by e-mail is a pleasant transition, plus it hones your typing skills. This is one of our favorite programs because it's one of the few pleasant activities available to the "technologically challenged."

3. After that, it's all downhill. You begin to feel crummy about yourself and your ability and even your sanity, and you strongly suspect that runny-nose six-year-old next door is no doubt "cutting and pasting" a trilogy electronically.

4. How is it all you gifted people have music and movies and every whim gratified by your computer while I don't have dip? Your mechanical pleasure is compounded by your iPod or Blackberry, although I'm convinced some of you are only pretending to talk on your cell phone so the rest of the world will think you're popular.

5. When something goes wrong with your computer, which it does more often than not, you know your day is going to go very badly, and you get that queasy feeling in your gut that only computers can produce. You fiddle with everything in sight, and on very rare occasions, you get the desired results. This makes people within earshot quite happy because they really didn't want to hear about your "#*&^$ computer" in the first place. Some will ask helpfully, "What did you do?" And of course you don't know, and you couldn't duplicate it if you were held at gunpoint.

6. If something is truly messed up and you go to the help selection, you will quickly learn it *doesn't*. Trust me on this.

I will admit, the computer is great for writing letters, or anything else you choose to write, once you discover those straight lines of a legal pad aren't needed anymore. Not only is a keyboard faster than writing by hand, but you don't have to redo the entire thing if you mess up. The Internet is a great reference tool, plus it has constant "breaking news," tons of "bloggers," as well as some most "titillating" selections.

Along with the rewards of ownership, comes responsibility. You may not be able to afford health insurance for yourself, but you have to have it for your computer, so you get anti-virus programs to prevent a bacteria bandit from slipping in the back door and spreading the sniffles around. Worse yet is a virus, and in either case, you end up calling your local computer guru, and getting through that is like repeating the SAT test in high school.

After I left one such guru several messages, he called and asked, "What sort of computer do you have?" I told him it was an old one. He then wanted to know the model and serial number. That was a rough one. I know where it is on my car, but I had to ask him for directions on this. He was a really good guru because he knew right where it was, even though he and my computer hadn't been in contact before. Before you know it, he'd gotten my name, address, and phone number as well as my birth date, the last four digits of my Social Security number, and my mother's maiden name. When he asked for the tracking numbers on my checking account and any medications I was taking as well as the number of milligrams of each, I demanded to know why he needed all this to fix my computer. His response: "Wait a minute, lady. That is a presumptuous statement because I never made the representation that I would fix your computer, and we ask all those questions because we think it's funny when people get really frustrated. That's why we're in the business."

At this point my computer isn't the only one with a headache. The good news is I can take care of mine, and it doesn't even involve Excedrin. After all, I can pull the plug. Now, that feels much better ...

THIS ONE IS FOR THE BIRDS

The Outer Banks is rich in a wide-ranging variety of birds, ducks, and geese. There are the year-round local types as well as the "tourists," who migrate up and down the Atlantic Flyway. The pelicans have returned, thanks to stricter environmental controls, and their daily shuttle flights over the ocean were a welcome sight after some lean years. Many of us learned as children, "A wonderful bird is the pelican. His bill can hold more than his belican" which, of course, enables them to wear smaller-size bikinis at the beach than their winged cousins.

The sea ducks are a delight to watch when they skim over the ocean, but my favorite little guys are the sandpipers at the water's edge that scurry to snag their food before the next wave. Their spindly legs carry them so quickly they look like feathers on speed!

The egret feeds in the calmer waters of the sound and is the most beautifully serene of birds, I think. And it's hard to forget the haunting cry of the loons when they voice their opinions. That is only the tip of the nest in terms of the winged components of the Outer Banks, which includes multiple varieties of seagulls. That crowd has an uncanny ability to beg a free lunch, and if you feed one, the entire gull nation shows up, even third world country gulls, and that's fine. I'd rather feed seagulls on the beach than pigeons from a park bench any day.

There are so many varieties of birds on the Outer Banks I wasn't overly concerned about baby crows, but this came up in a conversation one day out of the blue. A friend asked, "Why do you never see any baby crows?" I told her I hadn't been look- ing for them. The woman who posed this question knows the Outer Banks, plus she has an MBA from Harvard, and she was concerned about baby crows? I thought she would have been thinking about practi- cal matters like how to pull off a leveraged buyout or create the ultimate hedge fund. But no, she was concerned about the absence of baby crows.

She's a bright woman and an otherwise sane per- son, so I asked her why baby crows were important. She agreed that it wasn't in the same league with splitting the atom, but she wondered about it since she saw adult crows but never baby crows. I assumed she wasn't talking about young members of an Indian tribe, so I asked if they weren't the same thing as blackbirds. She said they were different birds, and I had my new fact for the day. I wondered about this and decided it was time to be on the lookout for baby crows. My "test market" was right there on the Outer Banks. Naturally I asked her where they would hang out. "What is their natural habitat?"

Here response was, "Oh, you know, the usual bird places."

I presumed they didn't frequent sports bars or shoe stores, but you never know. I suggested, "Maybe you've been looking for crows in all the wrong places."

She told me that was a song and the guy was "looking for love," not crows, "in all the wrong places."

I responded, "Yeah, and he found love so maybe we should contact him and put him on those baby crows."

She told me, "Just forget it."

Forget it! Are you kidding? It was definitely time to hone my detective skills, so I first went to my outdated *Webster's,* and sure enough, crows are different from blackbirds, and I hate it when she's always right. As it turns out, crows are "Any of several large non-migrating birds (esp. genus Corvus)... the raven, rook, and jackdaw are all crows. 2. (Rare) a crowbar. (Especially if you have a flat tire.) Next step of the investigation: talk to knowledgeable bird experts and start with a question that will knock their socks off, like, "Are there baby crows?" Predictable response, "Of course there are baby crows!" I then asked where they were, and you guessed it: they didn't know. I almost suggested they try to think of where they were the last time they saw them, like looking for a lost sock, but I decided against it.

I recently watched my copy of Alfred Hitchcock's *The Birds* and found it as scary as ever. Back when I showed it to my children, they thought it was "hilarious, not scary at all." One has to remember their generation grew up on *Eddie Scissor Hands,* graduated to *Friday the Thirteenth, Part One,* then *Jason the Jelly Person, Part Seven.*

When I watched *The Birds* again, I thought about baby crows. Hitchcock was the master of building credibility and suspense and ending with a bang. It starts so innocently when a random seagull attacks someone in a boat, dives right down and pecks a hole in her head. That is uncharacteristic seagull behavior, since most of them I've observed on the Outer Banks just hang out in grocery store parking lots or wait for a handout on the beach or splat up your car. I decided that seagull was an abused child.

Before you know it, Hitchcock has birds of all feathers flocking together, even adult and baby crows, and yes, blackbirds. These are bad birds with a distinctly negative attitude. Even though gas was much cheaper then, those birds managed to create enough havoc to get a gas station blown to smithereens, and it wasn't even about price. They just seemed to be quite irritated on general principle. Then it got so bad they were attacking regular people to the point they had to put up hurricane storm shutters to keep them out of their homes and block off their fireplaces with very pricey antique tables, but even that didn't work. Next thing you know, the birds overcrowded an outside school gym and pushed and shoved and broke in line, and that was before they attacked the necks of petrified school children and pecked the eyeballs out of people with otherwise pleasant facial features. In the final scene, the birds drove the inhabitants out of their home, even though all the mortgage payments had been made on time. Then they captured the turf, inside and out, complete with complimentary bird droppings no doubt. I thought that was a very unprofessional way to handle a foreclosure, plus it was totally unwarranted, but Hitchcock wrote it, I didn't.

After viewing *The Birds*, I wondered how they got so bad. Did some teenage birds get in with the wrong crowd? Were they "latchkey" birds, or were they doing drugs? Then I remembered reading that when the movie came out, they actually trained those birds to attack. I can't imagine how they would do that. *Lassie*, yes. A million birds, no. Maybe they ran ads in *The Tweety Times*, and every bird hungry for a shot at Hollywood and a bag of birdseed showed up. For all I know, "Rockin' Robin" got his start there, because they wrote a song about him. "Go, Rockin' Robin 'cause we're really gonna' rock tonight." Supporting cast, "All the little birdies in the bird bandstand."

Next obvious question: Once they trained those birds to be so mean, how did they un-train them so they could return to polite society? I'd like to think they really tried, but once you've achieved star status, you don't give it up easily. They probably had to snuff them, and they all flew off to birdie heaven, which may be the reason you see that feather floating around in *Forrest Gump*. This, of course, would explain why you never see any baby crows.

In retrospect, this theory probably won't fly. Wouldn't be the first time I've had to eat crow...

WHAT'S IN A
NAME?

If you are in search of Utopia, Tranquility, or simply a Mainstay, you will surely find kindred spirits in the Peaceable Kingdom, the Outer Banks. That Summer Place offers a "Raison D'Etre" for many and provides Downtime, a Retreat to Sanity for most. Once you find an Attitude Adjuster as effective as that, you will surely have found your Anchorage and realize you're in the Wright Place.

By way of explanation, the capitalized words in the previous paragraph, except the "Outer Banks," are real cottage names there. The names are fascinating, and they run the gamut from the philosophical to the whimsical with a lot of creativity in between.

No doubt there are many places where people name their summer homes, and it would be interesting to visit those, but I enjoyed uncovering the diversity of names that reflect the varied backgrounds and interests of those who made an investment on the Outer Banks.

Apparently some cottage owners first saw that as an Impossible Dream, and yet they Hadda-Havit and ended feeling No Regrets. Many opted to Sink or Swim and decided it was a Sound Choice to get a bank loan. That crowd obviously found it a Smart Move to achieve Solvent-Sea by going this route, possibly for Tax Porpoises, since it can be De-Duck-Table. One owner summed up this concept by naming his cottage Bank's Outer Banks. For others, Moma's Money made the difference between High Hopes and Finally Mine, At Last! A few must have ended Bankrupt with Empty Pockets, so I suppose the venture was an Albatross. Hopefully they are in the minority. I prefer to focus on those who viewed their cottages as a Labor of Love and created Almost Heaven in the Home That Love Built.

If you don't care for puns, you might as well skip to the next chapter because Outer Banks cottage names are frequently pun driven. Consequently, they can be great fun. Where else would you find Dunesberry or one who Dances with Waves? Sound Friends often UnCoyle there (the owner's name is Coyle), and find Ectasea in Seaclusion. Most who visit those shores know it is downright Beachy Keen to discover that Permanent Wave.

Many of the owners and visitors migrate from their Yankee Doodle Dune for a bit of Southern

Comfort. The warmth of the summer shores beckoned Jersey Jewel, Knob Hill East, and Minnesotan Thaw. There they found a Tarheel Treasure, where we were glad to see them Four Shore and usually asked Howya Dune? When they left we hoped to See-Ya-Round again and expect they took some Southern Memories with them.

We wish to interrupt at this juncture to find out what demented sort of person would name his cottage Sea Grits. Since we are personally from the South, we would naturally take offense at this sort of perverted name, except for the fact that we find it hilariously funny and tend to roll around on the floor in uncontrollable laughter with tears streaming down our cheeks when we see the name Sea Grits.

On a more serious note, some things never change, like the feeling you get when you kick through the surf on a warm summer night. That place was made for children—then, now, always. The Outer Banks connects generations. The cottage name Never Grow Up says it all, and I felt an affinity for cottages named Waterbugs, Sea Saw, and Duck, Duck Goose. I wasn't sure I wanted to meet Sun of a Beach, but I would have loved to meet the originator of the Crumblies, who is all grown up now. I asked one of our owners about the origin of that name, and he described it. He and his wife had truly looked forward to their vacation there, and this was absorbed by their very young daughter. When they crossed Currituck Sound, the co-pilot in the backseat exclaimed, "I just get the crumblies when I think about the beach!" I defy anyone to improve on that.

If you end in Duck, even with blindfolds on, you won't have to wonder where you are for long because so many of the cottage names there make a reference to ducks. You could have begun your journey in Kenny-Duck-Port at the Quack of Dawn for all we know. Once you reached this Duck Stop you would realize your trip wasn't a Wild Goose Chase. Clearly, This Duck's 4 U! And this doesn't stop with cottage names. I once spotted a delightful local license plate, which stated, "Quack NC."

Since we are on the subject of puns, we might as well introduce the subject of terns, since this seems to be as good a place as any to introduce the subject of terns. For the novices in the crowd, terns are those sea birds that look a lot like gulls but are smaller, so if you didn't know the difference, you might assume all the terns you see flying around are the runts of a gull litter, so to speak. The local terns were memorialized in cottage names such as Our Tern and Tern Too, but the greatest name of all is Tern Cote, which is not only a double pun, but coincidentally, also happened to be the name of our father's cottage.

Cottage names, especially the good ones, were frequently copied up and down the beach, and no one seemed to take offense. After all, imitation is the best sort of flattery. Our father did not share this view, however, when he discovered the second Tern Cote, a later imitator of the original. This may have been a happy accident, but we doubt it, and we happened to have hit teams stationed up and down the east coast from New York to Miami that were prepared to torch a cottage at a moments notice.

The cottage naming business covers it all, from those who must have gotten even with Jonah's Revenge and Golf Widow's Revenge to those in search of Good Vibrations there in the House of the Rising Sun. For the Conch Potato in search of Deck-a-Dance, there is Mac's Lounge where Happy Hour begins in Margaritaville and, no doubt, ends in the Recovery Room.

Even British royalty appeared to have gotten in on the act where the House of Stuart's vies with the White House for Ambience. The Prince of Whales found a King's Haven in his Clam Castle while America recalled Camelot. Today in America the Rightview—as in politically right of center—seems to have lost its luster after George W. Bush, which could spell Happy Days for the Democrats. I personally think America is in search of a leader-type-person who will bite the bullet and prove the Duck Stops Here.

If you happened to bring your pet with you on vacation, there are cottages that allow pets. The Happy Lab is one of them. Neither the Dog House nor the Salty Dog allows pets, so figure that out, and I have no idea if pets are allowed in the Cat's Meow. In other words, cottage names can be misleading. The Hokie House is anything but "hokie" judging by its outward appearance, so I suspect the owner of that cottage is a VPI graduate. The Dusty Duck

House, no doubt, just needs a good spring cleaning. I don't know who owns La Maison de Geezer, but it sounded like the owner could have been a good candidate for one of those motivational sessions they offer back on the mainland.

There was one group that never misled you with cottage names. The Olde Salt who landed there put you At Ease with a hearty Welcome Aboard to the Captain's Quarters, Wardroom, or Pilot House. (Hot tip for those without a Pinch of Salt in their veins—the Poop Deck is not a reference to a pet cottage.)

Northern Virginia visitors must have enjoyed Tysee's Corner, and I suspected the owner of Life's a Beach could be from Virginia Beach, but I couldn't confirm that. There is, however, one fact of which I was certain. You know where Richmond On The Sound originated, as described in a previous chapter.

On a happier note, musicians found a Symphony in the Key of Sea, while those with a bent toward the classics enjoyed Halcyon Days on those shores. Siren Song conjured memories of those sea nymphs who lured sailors to a watery grave centuries before the land pirates of Nags Head got wind of this concept and used a nag and lantern to achieve the same results.

"Carpe diem," when translated, means "seize the day," which we concluded was an early reference to Beach Week back when Latin was the "in" language and young Italians just out of school descended upon Mediterranean beaches to "vent," in search of lean, tan thighs, beer bongs, and the ultimate deck parties.

We really liked the way history repeated itself and personally thought "carpe diem" captured the Beach Week phenomenon very nicely.

If you are ever in a quandary about a name for your place in the sun, you could go for No Name or None of the Above, which are also real-live cottage names there. If you have a truly weird sense of humor, which some of us happen to have, you could name it Sea Grits of course.

We would suggest, however, you don't name it Tern Cote because if you do, you may Re-Grit it in the end!

"HOW'S THE WEATHER?"

When I worked as a reservationist, our most frequently asked question about a cottage, just after "How far is it from the ocean?" was usually a weather question. The callers often asked what the weather was doing, and when they came in to get their keys and directions, they often wanted to know what the weather would be for the upcoming week. There was only one answer to that question as far as I was concerned. "It's going to be a perfect beach week." How else *would* the weather be in God's country?

I am not embellishing the truth when I say this because, to me, the weather was almost always perfect on the Outer Banks, with the possible exception of an occasional hurricane. It could have been raining cats and dogs outside, or a nor'easter could have been pulling out the underpinnings of front line cottages as we spoke on the phone, and that was okay. I wouldn't have tolerated it for a minute on the mainland, but that sort of weather is perfectly acceptable there. There could have been a major thunderstorm that shut down our computers and provided the most spectacular light and sound show this side of a rock concert. Or it could have been a glorious beach day—and it usually was, in which case we would tell you the tanning index, at no extra charge, if we happened to know it. But every now and then we could get a hurricane churning up the coast with its eye focused on Hatteras, and that kind of weather could definitely detract from an otherwise perfect beach day.

I will say this for hurricanes: they have a way of getting the adrenaline pumping after the rates drop and the crowds leave. Hurricanes tend to be real attention-getters during the off-season when life slows down on the Outer Banks.

I have a history of making major moves under the worst possible conditions. That special gift didn't develop overnight, but rather was honed over many moves that culminated in the absolute pinnacle of perfection the week I moved to the Outer Banks, which was precisely the same week Hurricane Emily decided to move there too in August 1993.

My extensive research revealed there is only one thing normal people hate more than painting a house, and that is moving, so try on moving with a hurricane breathing down your back. I'm here to tell you, folks, that is the ultimate fun experience! Actually, I moved there just before Emily was supposed to hit. Anyone who has moved realizes this process involves at least 16,053 boxes. Once the boxes were emptied, I stacked them at the end of my very long driveway at the bottom of a very steep hill leading to my house. I didn't get wind of the imminent hurricane until just after the last box had been put on top of the pile. After all, who pays attention to the weather or anything else during a move?

There I was opening windows and unpacking accumulated treasures from past lives when I noticed my neighbors taping their windows and battening down the hatches. I decided to ask around. Sure enough, there she was, barreling up the coast with a bead on the Outer Banks, and Emily definitely had flair. Not only was she upgraded to a category three hurricane, packing winds well in excess of a hundred miles an hour, but all tracking devices indicated she planned to hit at high tide under a full moon, the worst of all possible circumstances. That was one hurricane with an agenda! I remembered the Ash Wednesday storm, or at least the remnants of it from my childhood, and that wasn't even a hurricane; it was a major spring storm augmented by a full moon and high tide. It devastated the Outer Banks.

I looked around at all the wonderful windows in my new place and the surrounding trees draped in Spanish moss just outside, and the very things I loved about my tree house were suddenly major liabilities. Tape for the windows was nonexistent by the time I got to the hardware store. The shelves had been wiped clean. I did get bottled water, and I had a supply of candles, packed somewhere, and a battery-powered radio. The cable wasn't hooked up, so there was no television, and the cable company wasn't about to do it then. When I got the cable guy on the phone, he basically said, "Later, lady, I'm leaving." I couldn't blame him.

I dragged some of the boxes back up the hill, cut them up, found my hammer and a few nails somewhere in the chaos, and got the windows covered. Then I called my neighborhood association and told them about the boxes. The woman who made things happen for Colington Harbour took care of it. How her maintenance people managed to get rid of all those boxes when they were already overloaded preparing for a major hurricane astounded me, but they did. After that they referred to me as "the Box Lady," and I have nothing but admiration for those people.

I followed Hurricane Emily on my radio, which is quite a different experience from the full-color extravaganza you get on the Weather Channel. It is one thing to *visually* track that low-pressure time bomb moving your way, but quite another to try to imagine *where* it is when they give you latitude and longitude on the radio and your atlas is packed somewhere in a box.

• • •

Lewis Grizzard, a Southern humorist, once posed the question, "How *long* would they go on about the weather?" Here's your answer, Lewis: The Weather Channel can "go on" about it twenty-four hours a day, and they do, but what those people live for is a trackable, low-pressure system. They can't track a tornado or waterspout, as much as they would love to, because those little devils pop up without warning and leave just as quickly. A hurricane, on the other hand, is high-drama, pure euphoria for the Weather Channel. You give those folks anything gusting over thirty-five miles per hour with a counter-clockwise drift and they will set their alarm clocks on early and turn it into a mini-series!

Emily, being the capricious hurricane she was, decided to visit during peak tourist season. I couldn't blame her for that. After all, everyone loves a great audience, and Emily was no exception. Once Emily built up a real head of steam, Dare County ordered a mandatory evacuation, and I have never witnessed a more professional operation. This was Patton at his best, devoid of ego.

Just in case some people missed the evacuation notices broadcast constantly on local television and radio stations, Dare County captured the attention of the beach crowd by mobilizing fire trucks with loud speaker systems that made it perfectly clear everyone was to evacuate the outer Banks *now*. As a result, thousands of families were directed to safety by the police and fire departments and back-up crews. The stop lights on the bypass were switched to flashing mode, and in the event some maverick decided to slip over to the west side to weather it out, those roads were blockaded. My radio predicted the storm surge would hit from the west, and I expect the county knew that. The counter-clockwise motion of the hurricane was expected to initially suck much of the water out of the sounds and inlets, and then return it tenfold with the impact of a tidal wave that would cause the ultimate destruction. Dare County definitely covered all the bases. For example, there are permanent "hurricane evacuation route" signs posted up and down the bypass. I personally view this as overkill because there are only two ways in or out along the same highway: "please exit north or south," so I figured if you got there in the first place, you already knew how to get back out. Maybe the county officials were accommodating the Type Bs and Code 8s (earlier chapter) when they posted those signs, but I'll say this for them: they know how to empty a danger zone as quickly as humanly possible. Admittedly, this takes quite some time during peak tourist season, even longer than waiting for the ice cream truck, but they get it done. Shortly after the evacuation was ordered, Dare County cut off all beer, wine, and liquor sales to discourage "hurricane parties," and Currituck County followed suit. The Outer Banks cleared out.

Admittedly, I left at the last possible moment. Somehow I couldn't get my gears in motion when it came to leaving the place I had only recently found again. I topped off my gas tank in torrential rain, and the fellow who ran out to take care of my bill glanced at the empty bypass and did a double take. His comment was spontaneous, "I can remember when it was like this all the time. Damn, I love this!" So did I. As I drove away, I noticed these words spray painted on the temporary plywood shield on a front door: "Would the last person to leave the Outer Banks turn out the lights?"

At the eleventh hour, whimsical Emily changed her mind and her course, leaving the majority of the Outer Banks untouched. Sadly, that eleventh hour turn didn't come in time to spare Hatteras, which suffered major infrastructural damage. Not only were homes, the schools, and businesses destroyed, but lives were altered irrevocably.

When it was over, Hatteras residents started wading through the water and mud to pick up the remnants. There were horror stories drifting up the banks from Hatteras, and that's when the locals dropped what they were doing and took care of their own. They went to Hatteras in droves to help out. When they weren't helping to rebuild, they were putting together fundraisers north of Hatteras for building materials, new books for the school library that was destroyed, whatever was needed. The local members of the National Surfers' Association moved there in full force and, quite possibly, donated more sweat equity than any group in an attempt to give a jumpstart to a place they loved and helped to make whole again. Emily certainly left tragedy in her wake, but she inadvertently left some silver lining in terms of neighbors helping neighbors.

Hurricanes happen. That sounds like a bumper sticker but isn't. They are a fact of life almost every fall along the east coast and the Gulf. So what! The Midwest endures tornados, and the west coast attempts to deal with earthquakes, and there is no way I would trade the Graveyard of the Atlantic for the San Andreas Fault. I lived in California long enough to realize those people had it all backward. Anyone with good sense should know the sun is not supposed to *set* over the ocean, so who needs that?

I expect the cynics in the crowd could make an issue of the Outer Banks if they chose to. After all, if a skinny little strip of sand is brazen enough to poke itself into a turbulent ocean, maybe it deserves what it gets. I don't buy that for a minute. For that matter, the Outer Banks is rarely hit by a hurricane, and I pray that trend continues, but you would never know that based on all the publicity it gets when it comes to memorable weather. One does sense the Outer Banks is a hot item when anchors of the major networks appear with multiple crews and satellite trucks, complete with lights and cameras, to report the action to the rest of the world.

For those in the know, the most memorable weather is delivered to your doorstep almost daily there, as a result of that rare juxtaposition of the land and sea. That combination produces glorious weather most of the time, but every now and then you get weather so spectacular it is worth writing home about.

On of our visitors phrased it best when he turned in his keys on the way back home. We apologized for the rain during part of his past week with us.

His response was immediate, "Don't worry about it. The worst weather here is always better than the best weather back home." How could I possibly add to that?

So from now on, if you happen to ask me, "How's the weather there?" I may borrow a line from one of my favorite Willie Nelson songs and tell you: It's "Close Enough to Perfect For Me."

BREAKING NEWS: HURRICANE GORDON

When Hurricane Gordon was breathing down our necks, our office, like most businesses on the beach, was closed in anticipation of the blow. Consequently, I had the opportunity to watch the events unfold on the Weather Channel and record Gordon's saga. It may seem bizarre to include this now, but I think it's an interesting contrast between this guy and Hurricane Emily in the previous chapter. Mainly, I'm a sucker for weather stories and breaking news, even if it was in 1994!

. . .

(November 18, 1994)

People frequently talk about the weather in other locales to pass the time of day. When people on the Outer Banks discuss the weather, they are usually dead serious. At this writing, Hurricane Gordon is stalled off our coast approximately one hundred miles south of Cape Hatteras, and believe me, this weather is being discussed, not only by the locals, but by national television as well. Of course, the Weather Channel has a full-color extravaganza covering every twist and turn, and weirdo Gordon is full of those. As the waves continue to build and encroach more and more, there is an extraordinary amount of discussion going on around us.

Gordon started out so low key I don't think anyone took him seriously. He was a tropical storm for too long and, consequently, missed all the good press releases. At first he just wallowed around doing tropical storm-type things, and nobody gave him the time of day, not even the Weather Channel. Next thing you know, he developed an agenda and devastated part of Florida. He then flip-flopped back across Florida for good measure, wreaking havoc all the way, whereupon he decided to head for the warm waters of the Gulf Stream in search of hurricane status and high visibility. Now I ask you, was this guy having an identity problem or what? Gordon was probably a "child left behind." For all I know he could have been going through that male midlife crisis thing, and if that was the case, we should have sent him a sports car, because he was definitely too close for comfort. I personally thought Gordon was a hurricane in need of therapy, and once low-pressure systems get named, I tend to assign personality traits to them.

So Gordon was stalled just off our coast, basking in all his macho hurricane glory, and we learned early that morning that the Outer Banks was expected to take a direct hit. That, thanks to yet another major change in this weirdo's course. And they say *women* are indecisive! All the while the ocean was building, and TV camera crews from everywhere but riot-torn countries were descending on the Outer Banks to relay the devastation and pure drama of the moment to the rest of America.

Those fun-seeking camera crews in search of something to do focused on Kitty Hawk, where four cottages were toppled by the waves, with all the bits and pieces that create a home being tossed like so many Legos into the surf. National television showed those same four cottages being sucked into the ocean over and over again, so if you weren't watching closely, the perception was created that homes up and down the beach were dropping like flies. That was not the case at all, and they failed to mention the fact that those four dwellings were already doomed, completely undermined by previous storms. They were ready to go at the drop of a hat, a minor nor'easter, possibly even a spring rain.

Hey, I don't blame the news teams or camera crews. Sensationalism sells. I only wish those people would visit the Outer Banks just once, for a real vacation rather than in a work capacity when disaster threatens. I think it would do them a world of good.

I turned on WAVY-TV 10 out of Hampton Roads at noon to get the latest update. Gordon seemed to enjoy playing his hide-and-seek game that was driving the experts nuts. His mercurial path was baffling the hurricane gurus, and I almost felt sorry for the meteorologist doing the noon report. That poor guy was stuck with the day shift, that day of all days, and he was expected to give us a valid prediction. So he began by saying, "We have five computer projections of the possible courses Gordon can take. I will give you my choice, after this..." When the commercial came on, I was thinking, *Place your bets! Place your bets!*

I don't blame that weather person a bit. After all, the director of the National Hurricane Center in Miami described Gordon as "The most difficult complex system we've had to deal with." How could that poor weather person tell us Gordon's direction when even Gordon didn't have a clue where he was going?

Thankfully, Gordon made yet another switch mid-afternoon. He completed a turn to the south and exited the Outer Banks, which led me to believe he may have gotten counseling after all! Any decent counselor will tell you, you just don't mess with God's country. I am convinced of that. Gordon definitely had problems from the beginning. Not only was he a late bloomer, but he was a late baby who came crashing onto the scene in November, well past the usual hurricane season. On top of that, this sad fellow never knew the difference between right and left, much less the difference between north, south, east, and west. Now I ask you, would you take this guy home to meet your family?

Actually it wasn't Gordon's fault. He was an unhappy victim of circumstance, a victim of the hurricane experts who apparently thought it would be a nifty idea to assign male names to half the hurricanes in an attempt at sexual equality. I assume this was their intent, and I appreciate the thought, but as I recall, women are working for equity in the marketplace, not the hurricane department. Female hurricanes do a bang-up job of breaking glass windows and doors, but I'm not convinced this development has enabled women to break some of those elusive "glass ceilings."

If you hurricane experts want a real hurricane with a definable course, give it a memorable female name, and cut it loose. I'm talking hurricanes that take a straight path for the jugular, make the hit, and then go about their business. That's sensible. Better yet, it's predictable, which would make your jobs easier.

"Hell hath no fury like a woman scorned." You know that and I know that, but if you doubt it, I would ask you, when was the last time you saw a "scorned" woman take an *undetermined* course? If you can find one, I want to hear about it.

Meanwhile, don't send a man to do a woman's job!

THE HARDWARE STORE AND THE BLOB

Every spring there is an annual migration of property owners to the Outer Banks. That starts well before the season cuts loose, and the owners flock there in droves to open up their cottages, air them out, turn the water on, and take care of any problems that may have developed over the winter. Of course, the owners who didn't drain their pipes may have had to visit over the winter to take care of broken pipes.

Anyone who has ever owned property on the Outer Banks can tell you there is only one store that is indispensable there, and that is the hardware store. I'll bet you guessed the grocery store or the gas station, or some might be prone to go for the liquor store. No, the indispensable hardware store is that destination for the homeowner that's slam full of tools and screws and widgets for any occasion, as well as hot tubs to draw the crowds.

I think this phenomenon may be especially pronounced on the Outer Banks because salt air produces rust, and between that and high winds and high water at times, the expiration date on integral parts of a cottage can occur sooner than expected.

If you think I'm kidding about hardware stores, I have proof that I'm not. Some time ago I sold advertising for several radio stations on the Outer Banks, and the owner of these stations, as well as all members of our staff, were amazed at this particular event. Our biggest client was Ace Hardware, and our stations did a number of "remotes" for Ace, which translates: the station would do a live show from the store that usually lasted about three hours. The jazzy radio van that carried all the equipment to transmit the show had the station name emblazoned on it so it couldn't be missed when parked in front of the store. The event was advertised often and well in advance on the stations, and a DJ would announce on site, play music, often interview customers live on the air, and constantly remind people to stop by. There was a festive atmosphere, and more times than not, they'd serve hot dogs and hamburgers, sometimes pizza, and always soft drinks to the crowds. This was all free to the public as a way of thanking them for stopping by, and they were encouraged to shop around the store.

Those were fun events, and if the weather allowed, they often had cookouts in the parking lot, sometimes a band, and there was definitely a party atmosphere. But the reaction to this Ace Hardware "remote" in the fall on the Outer Banks was proof positive that hardware *is* indispensable in that environment. Advertised well in advance, Ace was throwing an "End of Season Customer Appreciation Sale." That was prior to Home Depot, and the property owners were there to close up for the winter, plus the local home owners loved a deal as much as anyone. Everything in the store was reduced dramatically. There were hot dogs and hamburgers cooked on the store's best-selling grill, "priced just right" for the occasion, and large carts were conveniently located for loading up the deals. People were lined up ten to twelve deep at every cash register, and unless you got there early you couldn't park in an eight block radius. When it was all over, the customers were well fed and thrilled with their "steals." Ace was particularly pleased, and we all agreed that was the most swinging Saturday night we'd ever seen on the Outer Banks in the fall. What did I tell you about those hardware stores?

There is one hardware store fact that applies to every human being consistently throughout history. If you don't believe me, look at the inscriptions carved in the pyramids they've discovered. The hieroglyphics were actually designed to fool regular people like you and me, because all the while, we thought they were just pictures of people with sideways faces, men who were wearing skirts that clearly weren't kilts, and a lot of birds. But we're just your average lay people, so what do we know? As it turns out, they assembled a group of anthropologists, geologists, and forensic scientists, network and satellite news, plus Henry Kissenger at "an undisclosed location." This of course, was a natural for Henry, and the meeting was unusually productive. The secret in the pyramids revealed the Mother of all Murphy's Laws, and it is this: "No matter what your project is, you will make more than one trip to the hardware store."

You might wonder why this would be the one pearl of wisdom they would choose to pass down through antiquity, but I think you have to imagine the circumstances when it was inscribed, plus it *is* true—the pyramids never lie. You have to picture those poor, starved, whipped slaves being forced to build this pharaoh's tomb, even when they'd never met him personally. The fellow mixing the mortar with an early, crude stirring utensil tells the foreman, "Hey, man, we need a lot more bags of mortar mix, and one of the wheels on my wheelbarrow is falling apart again. You'd think they'd make 'em with spokes." The foreman was a notch above your regular slave, and he cared about his men, plus he was a higher up in the Pyramid Builders Local 103, so he had clout. He told one of the men to make a run to the hardware store to get a ton of mortar and to see if they had any spoke wheels in stock. He said the guy could take his truck, and he told him to put it on the pharaoh's account. "Don't worry about it. He's dead and will never know the difference." (Of course you and I know he didn't have a truck in ancient Egypt—he was a slave.)

So, making more than one trip to the hardware store is a fact of life, and it has been that way since the beginning of time. Get used to it, because if you don't live next door to a hardware store, you'd better gas up right now if you have any kind of project planned. Case in point: I remember one delightful cottage owner when I was doing inspections on rental properties. He was a cardiologist, and I've found that many doctors are quite dexterous, and I've known several who paint or build furniture as a hobby, for example. This particular doctor was obviously excited about something he was going to build in his cottage, and he told me he had everything for the job. He said he'd planned the project from beginning to end, had been to the hardware store and had everything he needed. I told him he thought he did but that he'd make several more trips. This was my way of giving him a personal testimonial on my home projects, but he insisted he was all set and wanted me to see all the widgets he'd purchased. He was really proud of this. I told him I'd probably run into him at the end of the season in the same capacity, and I'd check with him then. I did see him at the end of the season and, of course, asked him how many more trips he'd made to the store, and he turned away and mumbled, "Three or four." I asked him to speak up. He ended agreeing with me about that Murphy's Law of hardware stores.

I've found that many do-it-yourselfers have had "unforgettable" hardware experiences. My personal favorite stemmed from the time my partner and I replaced the floor in a small hall and found an unusual product to seal the space where the floor abuts the wall. There were any number of products on the market to choose from, and our pick of that new crop was one I called "the blob," designed by sadistic chemistry people with nothing but time on their hands. It came in a tube, and I never knew you could package a sense of humor in a tube, but "the blob" had it, because it worked through three highly evolved stages, and after we'd broken a serious sweat, it said, "Ha-ha! Gotcha!"

It came out white and creamy from its tube, looked innocent enough to be mistaken for some kind of face cream or hair conditioner. Don't be fooled because it is used to insulate cracks and crevices. The directions were explicit: "Apply a thin line." They should have said "microscopic line." Now here's your chemistry hoot of the day. Stage one: "Apply a thin line around the crevices to be sealed." Stage two: "When the air hits it, it puffs up like Styrofoam, which makes it a great insulator." Stage three: "It gets harder than a cinder block."

So my partner was in the hall applying a "thin line" around the spaces between the sub floor and the walls. Stage two was actually the most fun, and I watched until I thought the puffing up thrill was over. About three minutes later, he called out and sounded most concerned, as he announced, "It's still growing!" I went to see, and sure enough, he was starting to be surrounded by that blob, and the hall was shrinking by the minute. We made a quick decision to pull that goo off. Too late, because stage three, the cinder block stage, had already started working. "Gotcha!"

So my dutiful partner pulled out his toolbox, started hammering and chiseling, and quickly discovered a cinder block would kill to be that hard! A diamond might have worked, but since we didn't have any fresh diamonds handy, a chisel and hammer had to do. I did my fair share of hammering and chiseling and, meanwhile, I was thinking about that stage two where it puffed up, and it brought back memories of the strawberry fluff recipe I read as a young bride that was described as "a perfect light compliment to end a dinner with special guests."

I'll be the first to admit that men and women think quite differently, and I understand that has a lot to do with testosterone and estrogen. So while my buddy was breaking a sweat hammering and chiseling, I was recalling that stupid strawberry fluff recipe because the similarities between that and the goo were striking. The illustration featured a long-stemmed glass filled with a fluffy pink substance that actually looked appetizing, and the fluff was topped with a strawberry, leaves intact. It indeed sounded like "a perfect light compliment to end a dinner with special guests." Plus, you could tell it was really gourmet because they left the leaves on the strawberry on top.

So I made this stuff, and that's when I discovered the puffing-up stage, just like the goo in the hall. Stage two in this mess involved a bunch of strawberries, some egg whites, sugar, and an ingredient I must have left out. The catalyst for this concoction was an electric mixer, and once it was beaten to the consistency described, I was to put it in a long-stemmed glass, and top it with a fresh strawberry with leaves, of course. The recipe should have started out, "How many large bowls do you personally own?" After beating the contents, I transferred half the mixture to another large bowl, because it outgrew the original bowl and still hadn't reached the "proper consistency." I alternated beating both bowls, and it kept growing without achieving the desired results. Five large bowls and a bottom refrigerator drawer later, bingo! I had it. The only problem was, I ended with Pepto-Bismol "clouds," but the color was even more disgusting than that of the original medicine, which was designed to aid indigestion, not create it. Besides, it tasted like bird barf. I couldn't even find a trashcan liner large enough to get rid of that mess, and a thirty-gallon didn't get it. I did get rid of it in some rather innovative ways, and got out the remaining strawberries, which turned out to be "a perfect light compliment" to any meal.

The similarities between that crevice "blob" and the strawberry fluff were obvious to me. If I had just gotten those chemistry folks to put a tiny bit of hardener, mixed with some fluff in a tube, I'd have had a more manageable product that was cost effective when I was in a mode to insulate. So what if there was a yucky pink line around the edge of the sub floor? It wouldn't have mattered because I was going to cover it.

That concoction could actually be a weapon of war with enough hardener in it. Think about it. "Draw a thick line" around those tanks, and by gosh, you've immobilized an entire platoon! "Sorry, Rommel, you're not going anywhere today." Or find some terrorists wandering around the rocks in Afghanistan, or wherever they're wont to wander, and you could put down a line in the sand, but this time it would have clout.

It might be a hard sell to the military in strawberry fluff pink, but you could probably whip it up with some prunes and a little green food coloring, add that hardener, and you've got it, camouflage blob. Simply name it, Just Desserts.

FOR THE LOCALS

I realized after living through a winter or two on the Outer Banks that I qualified as a "local." That wasn't the same as being a "native," but it sufficed, although I did feel I should get some points for all my past spent there. After all, when did it get retroactive?

The Outer Banks is rapidly becoming a more year-round sort of place. The smart money is on the fall months when the rates drop, the hordes leave, the weather is incomparable, and the fishing is at its best. The old timers have known that all along. Thanksgiving is tremendously popular, and cottages are booked months in advance in anticipation of that. Between peak season and Thanksgiving, people without children in school take advantage of the glorious fall months. Christmas on the Outer Banks is getting big, and at New Year's, partial and full weeks appear to be coming in vogue. But once January sets in, it gets a bit chilly between the nor'easters and the job market, when half the work force is out of work in an economy based on tourism. That situation continues until spring, and once summer kicks in, the cycle starts over. But the winter months are lean, and those who stick it out earn the title "local," which is valued around those parts.

The compensation for the lean months lies in a close-knit community and in the landscape. The ocean can switch from serene to stormy in a matter of minutes. That's when the wind shifts, the water changes color, and the impact of salt air in your face can take your breath away. But the ocean doesn't do much for the job market when there are more people "between opportunities" than gainfully employed, or employed at all.

The way I look at it, *The Coastland Times* and *The Sentinel* should try a whole new approach to their "Help Wanted" sections during the cold months. If half of the locals are looking there for a job opportunity, they need to refocus. They should be reading the funnies and horoscopes in *The Virginian-Pilot* instead. At least that way they might be able to get a laugh out of it! I doubt I would ever find ads like the following ones in any of the papers listed, but I would love, just once, to find this sort of ad in some newspaper:

Managerial Position

150K to start. Fortune 200 Company. Entry level. On-the-job training will enable you to realize your full potential with this world-class corporation within a few short weeks. If you can smile, answer the phone, and are a high school graduate or less, this may be *your* career opportunity! E.O.E.

Or, if you really want a good hoot over your breakfast cereal, try this one on:

Immediate Need

499 warm bodies to guide Airhead Technologies, Inc. in this century. All you have to do is show up. If you don't call us, we'll call you. Full company benefits include hospitalization, orthodontia, laser surgery, facelifts, or compensation for whatever ails you. E.O.E.

I'll bet you're cracking up right now over these fun ads. You might as well stop laughing because if you open *The Coastland Times* or *The Sentinel* to the Help Wanted section you're more likely to find:

Sewing Machine Operators—Third Shift

Master's degree in Industrial Engineering required. Ph.D. preferred. The successful candidate will possess:

1. Knowledge of state-of-the-art American, German and Japanese industrial machines for straight stitching (lockstitch and chain stitch), slipstitch and bartack required to the extent of unaided ability to disassemble/reassemble totally in order to maximize machine up-time.

2. Twelve years progressive experience
and managerial growth.

3. Interpersonal skills to motivate
fellow employees on third shift.

4. Must be able to convey themes of Maslow,
Hawthorne, Parkinson, Murphy, Peter's
Principle and Theories X, Y, and Z to
experienced operators and trainees.

5. Must be adept in developing and
maintaining group adherence to
aggressive training curve.

Send brief job history and salary requirements to:

P.O. Box 0000
Forget It, USA 23510
E.O.E.

If you interview for that third shift position, you will probably find the other 498 candidates who interviewed before you—the other ones with Ph.D.s and hands-on experience—were also twenty-five years old, and like you, look like a young Harrison Ford or Meryl Streep. I size it up this way: the candidate who gets that job, no doubt, flosses more than you do and has been on *Meet the Press* or *Larry King Live*. Take heart. If you continue to laugh at the classified ads daily, you will surely find gainful employment. Or something. After all, they are all Equal Opportunity Employers.

No doubt about it. The job market reflects the trend of corporate belt tightening, but the job market on the banks is mainly a seasonal thing, which really can't be compared to the norm. People hurt there in a different way, or some of them do, so this chapter is on me, for the "locals."

When the winter months grow lean and the Help Wanted ads get sparse, any diversion will do. While you are reading this, I'd be willing to bet there are hundreds of people right there who are screening the classifieds for a pet cemetery or looking for that unique personal that speaks to them. "SWF seeks quiet candlelit dinners, winter walks on the beach, and sharing erotic toys with Christian nonsmoker."

Actually the Personals were often more fun than the front pages, which devoted multiple columns to the most recent DUIs. If you're gainfully employed, you have the luxury of watching Saturday morning cartoons or picking sand spurs out of your socks when you're off work. If you are "between opportunities," I have a better idea than looking for shells on the winter beach, because if you are in search of a roof to keep you dry, where are you going to put them anyway?

Has it ever occurred to you to start your own business? You would hardly be the first person on the Outer Banks to do that, and there are some very successful entrepreneurs on that beach. There are many needs, and there may just be a niche that's right for you. Consequently, I devised this free ad kit with descriptions of various businesses. Any one of these advertisements, run under Services in the classifieds, could bring in some much-needed money.

There are any number of opportunities, and selling your services is helped if you can grab the reader/buyer's attention. Admittedly, not all jobs are terribly appealing, such as pumping septic tanks, but they pay the rent and can be lucrative. If you need money to get started, it's a good idea to prepare a well thought-out business plan, take it to the bank, and pray. Feel free to use a sample ad from this kit in your business plan if you think it could be helpful.

Firewood for Sale

$55 per cord. $25 if we use your trees. Call 261–9328.

If It Don't Go Down, Call Brown

Tired of septic tank backup? Tired of going to the bathroom in your own back yard? Maybe it's time you called Brown to flush out your problems.

"We take everybody else's,

We might as well take yours."

Because a Flush Beats a Full House Every Time

Call 441–0083

(What bank wouldn't float a loan for a business like that?)

North Carolina Barbecue

Chopped Fresh Daily. Send Someone You Hate. "We drop 'em, and we chop 'em." Don't miss Sweet Revenge on the bypass, 11 MP.

Heads Up!

Heads on med. shrimp—$6.95/lb.

Heads off med. shrimp—$8.95/lb

7-day-old shrimp, any size: $10.95—to you—to cart them off. 255–6394.

Does Your Drinking Water

Taste like yesterday's aardvark? Cool Clear Water offers an alternative. Call 1-800-H2O-COOL for information on franchise opportunities.

If You're Getting Strung Out in the Neck, You're Going to Die Soon.

Timeshare burial plots could be the answer for you! Share A Grave offers, for a limited time only, reduced prices on marble headstones (fluorescent lettering optional) *plus* plastic flowers on Mother's Day. Adjacent pet cemetery and cypress trees can be arranged. For more information on your final resting place, please call 1-800-DIE-SOON. Our operators are standing by, so call before it's too late.

Check Out This New American Classic! The "BCT"

Bacon, cabbage and tomato on wheat, rye or pumpernickel, the new approach to an old favorite and perfect for those crisp fall months. Sink your teeth into this one and wake up your taste buds as you crunch your lunch. Only available at McBob's. Dine in/Take out. 8 MP Bypass.

Have You Tried the Ultimate "Rush"?

Bungee jumping without a cord! We are licensed to train you in the art of Bungee Jumping. Featured, This Week Only, Buy One, Get One Free!

$65 first jump with cord.

Cordless second jump free!

Our motto: "Go out with a bang, not a whimper!" Located across from the big hill on the bypass.

The Beached Whale

The *only* place to shop for the full-figured woman on the Outer Banks. We shop international markets, and Wanchese, to bring you classic contemporary designer lines in beach, cruise and tent wear. On the Beach Road, of course. 16 MP.

Has Your Home Been Tested for Radon?

Are Ninja Turtles showing up in your toilet? The simple Chernobyl test can put your worst fears to rest. Our bonded radon professionals can give you the bottom line.

"When radon is the game,

Chernobyl is the name."

If you suspect you have a radon problem, call Chernobyl for quiet, efficient testing. Call today: 255–6697.

Attention: Rodanthe Surfers

Sick of those "No Parking" and "No Trespassing" signs that keep you off the beach? No problem!

Spray-On Whiteout

Will take care of those nuisance signs. 15-ounce can only $5.95. Money-back guarantee for up to fifty signs. Available at most surf shops.

Okay, if you don't get that bank loan, you may want to look at these helpful ads:

Double-Wide Priced to Sell

Stove, refrigerator, indoor plumbing, washer/dryer hookup (next door). Within walking distance to pawn shop. Furniture stays. So does cat. Only $9,500. Call quick: 480–7198.

Or if you want employment that will focus on your many attributes, you may want to consider:

If You're Built Sorta' Like a Brick Pagoda, Mermaids Wants You!

Clean table tops and dancing poles for exotic dancing in Currituck County. Great benefits. Call Mel for an interview: 491–2375.

No doubt, there will be a few people who won't take advantage of these helpful suggestions. After all, there is a segment there that ain't going to buy Madison Avenue, even "for a limited time only." I once spotted a live one on the bypass, and his bumper sticker said it all: "Work is for people who don't fish." I bet Madison Avenue never thought of that one. I did notice the fellow driving that wheezing old car with the sticker looked happier than a pig in slop, probably because he never read a Help Wanted ad in his life.

Okay, I'll come clean: If you're a "local," you don't have to actually pay for these valuable suggestions. However, feel free to send donations, you know, to cover the rent and all.

CRIME WITHOUT PUNISHMENT

The Outer Banks prides itself on its rich history, clean beaches, and yes, low crime rate. Thinking back on it, maybe we should have called the police after all...

It started innocently enough just before Christmas. I was going to make Christmas cookies, as is my usual custom. The only problem was, I couldn't find my rolling pin. My kitchen was well organized, and I knew precisely where my rolling pin was, or I thought I did. It wasn't there, so after I searched the kitchen contents, I called my next-door neighbor and good friend to borrow hers. "Sure let me get it," she replied. She called back perplexed, saying, "I just used it last week, and I can't find it anywhere." We got a laugh out of this and both decided to buy one the next day, since

Christmas was coming and we were in the cookie phase, prior to "the goose getting fat."

On a lark, I called a great friend, who also happens to be a good cook. "Stephen, it is six seventeen p.m., do you know where your rolling pin is?"

His obvious response was, "What?"

I explained the situation, and he said he surely knew where his was and asked me to hold on. Wonder of wonders, he couldn't find it in the usual place, and he was intrigued; he said he'd call me back after a search. You guessed it. His was gone too. I told him I thought the culprits were working south to north and advised him to call any friends living north of him and tell them to get their rolling pins out of harm's way. We got a large chuckle out of this.

The only problem with Stephen is that he never forgets anything—not zip codes, not phone numbers. No detail is forgotten, not even some of the things I said in jest. The following summer he was doing security inspections on vacation rental properties, as I was, to determine if any items were missing after the guests left. At some point, he reported to me a particularly bad Saturday with a number of items missing from rental cottages. I asked him what he'd found missing, and he responded, "Oh you know, the usual: bedroom phones, remote controls, and … rolling pins." This thing began to take on a life of its own, and I dubbed it "The Insidious Rolling Pin Scam."

Of course, being the good investigative reporter I am, I decided to ask around. I only interviewed real rolling pin user-types, and sure enough, it became evident those wooden pins were disappearing like flies in the dead of winter. I already knew the perpetrators of that dastardly deed were working south to north. I first thought it could be termites gobbling up rolling pins, but upon further investigation, I ruled out that theory because any termite worth his salt would always eat the underpinning of the house, then go for the house, save the kitchen cabinets and drawers for last, and probably never go for the biggest bite of all, the rolling pin. Every rolling pin user I interviewed still lived in the home they originally bought or leased, and when the interview was conducted, the premises were in about the same condition as when they moved it. The other thing they had in common was the fact that a substantial majority had not seen their rolling pin for years.

If you think this is small potatoes, think again. For all I know, that could have been happening all over the United States, working south to north. If that was the case, it could have global implications, and it could well have been occurring from the South Pole to Mrs. Claus's kitchen. Before it was over, rain forests would be hacked down for wood to replace that volume of rolling pins, which would lead to over wash from soil with the consistency of loose grits. That, in turn, would lead to flood, famine, disease, starvation, and serious global unrest, resulting in big-time war.

Before you start bragging about "the low crime rate" on the Outer Banks, you should remember this story. Maybe we should have called the police in the first place.

MERRY CHRISTMAS!

By the time you have experienced the winter beach to the point you can almost predict where the next breaker of the next nor'easter will crash on the dune line, it's time to get ready for Christmas. That's when sailboat masts are strung with lights and wreaths are hung on front doors and almost everything that floats.

If you pay close attention, you may catch a glimpse of Santa, all decked out in his Santa suit, kicking through the sand at the surf's edge with a couple of elves in tow, his tennis shoes in one hand. That's right folks, *Santa really wears tennis shoes,* and I've got a picture to prove it!

What could possibly spoil this picture? I'll tell you what. It's those snooty overkill Christmas letters you get from the people you never heard from the other 364 days of the year. You know the ones I'm talking about. Those insufferable yuletide messages that are printed on red or green cardstock, seriously festooned with holly and berries, all designed to provide the ideal backdrop so you can truly appreciate the incredible achievements of these incredible overachievers. And that's before you get to the part about what little Joey did on the soccer team last year, should you stay awake long enough to absorb that.

Why do these people choose Christmas to send the sort of "happy gram" that leaves you feeling like you just spent your own last year wallowing in a bucket of warm spit?

I decided it was about time to get rid of this sick Christmas syndrome (SCS). So for those recipients who were left feeling like cold grits last Christmas, here's your answer for the upcoming Christmas. This is an all-inclusive sort of Christmas letter, complete with handy check-off boxes to save you time during the hectic holiday season. We have also provided enough space for you to be briefly eloquent should you decide to add a personal touch. The main thing to remember at the end is *always* say, "May you enjoy happiness and prosperity in the New Year." That's really important. Gives it validity, you know.

Dear family and friends,

    Merry Christmas! ❏

    Happy Chanukah! ❏

    Season's Greetings! ❏

    Here's the dirt! ❏

There are carols in the air, and as we relax next to a crackling fire, we realize it's again time to rub your noses in our success and share

    1. Our children's exceptional accomplishments   ❑

    2. The story of our obscene wealth   ❑

    3. Our world travels   ❑

As we prepare for the season's festivities, we look back over the past year and are thrilled that_____ (fill in name of husband, boyfriend, "special friend") not only was featured on the cover of *Time* as "Man of the Year" but also won the coveted Nobel Peace Prize. His talents and energy are boundless, and his latest interest is

    1. Transoceanic swimming   ❑

    2. Crop dusting   ❑

    3. Blowing his nose   ❑

Meanwhile,_____(fill in name of wife, girlfriend or "special friend") has stayed busy since completing her post-doctoral work this year by chairing the Junior League Cotillion, working as corresponding secretary for Who's Who in America and serving on several bank and mental health boards, as well as

    1. Filming a documentary for *National Geographic*   ❑

    2. Teaching bungee jumping   ❑

    3. Starting a worm farm   ❑

You can imagine our delight when our young-est won *America's Funniest Home Video* with his very own video of a neighbor's house in flames, which he orchestrated from beginning to end! We rushed home from Maui just in time to be with him on national television when he was awarded his prize money. Our little elf is now investing his prize by forming a syndicate with

1. Warren Buffet ❑
2. Bill Gates ❑
3. SpongeBob ❑

In the interim our oldest, a Rhodes Scholar, who recently graduated summa cum laude from

1. Oxford ❑
2. Harvard ❑
3. Slippery Rock U. ❑

spent a quiet summer studying Mother Teresa's work to learn how the other half lives.

Last spring we all managed to take time from our hectic schedules to enjoy a two-week cruise down

1. The fjords of Norway ❑
2. The Amazon ❑
3. The Dismal Swamp ❑

This proved to be a wonderful family adventure that will always be cherished.

In early summer we couldn't resist an invite to go on safari in Kenya, where we landed a lone wildebeest. He now adorns the east wall of the den, overseeing the pool and tennis courts just outside.

Thankfully, our frenzied pace slowed last fall and afforded us some reflective moments aboard our ketch, the *Smell Me*, at our place in Martha's Vineyard. We were thrilled when

1. Chris Buckley ❏
2. Ted Turner ❏
3. Gomer Pile ❏

_____(fill in your choice) surprised us with a visit and showed us the finer points of navigation.

Our holiday celebrations began early this year with the usual round of parties and charity functions, but the highlight of the season was our family's starring role in *The Nutcracker*. What fun we had hamming it up!

We would be remiss if we didn't mention our darling

1. Welsh Corgi ❏
2. Lhasa Apso ❏
3. Ferret ❏

Chloe, who sleeps contentedly by the fire. Little does she know that she will find extra treats in her stocking for again taking "Best in Show" at our annual winter carnival.

As we gather 'round our glittering tree, we take a moment to reflect on the true blessings of this joyous season, the love of family and friends. We are so looking forward to hearing from you and are eager to hear

What you are driving	❑
If you plan to get a life	❑
If you can top this	❑

Time to carry on with the festivities! May you enjoy happiness and prosperity in the New Year.

Hugs,	
Bootsie and Scooter	❑
Victoria and Duncan	❑
Tammy Sue and Jo Bob	❑

MIDWINTER BLUES ON THE BANKS

Along about mid-February when you have just about had it with winter and are ready for spring to kick in, it's time for ACC Basketball. I have personally observed many people who want February to fall off the calendar, but some optimists in the crowd just wish it had been short-sheeted a few more days. In terms of February, I'm all for keeping Valentine's Day, and I'm totally neutral on Groundhog Day, but I've never been neutral about Atlantic Coast Conference Basketball, which reaches a fever pitch about mid-February and gives the month a reason to be, not to mention the March Madness that follows.

This is a highly biased account that states right up front that ACC Basketball is the finest basketball in the stratosphere, so you don't have to mess around with watching any other basketball if you elect to see pure talent at its best. For starters, college players aren't paid, or at least they aren't supposed to be, and I find it refreshing to find any athlete who isn't paid these days.

The ACC frequently dominates "The Final Four," that nationwide college basketball showdown, which often results in the ultimate national wins for ACC teams.

I was originally a football nut, and my son is totally responsible for getting me hooked on basketball. This started when he was too little to reach the net, even though he thought he could. I saw him drag the stepladder out of the garage one day and open it up, right under the basketball goal. I started to stop him, but I wanted to see where it was going, and he was doing so well I couldn't bring myself to end it. He checked the ladder to make sure it was secure and where he wanted it, then he climbed to the top with his basketball and dropped it in the hoop. He looked elated. "So that's what it feels like. Cool!"

I still remember his endless midwinter practice at the top of the driveway. He'd put off coming inside as long as possible and then would run in with blue lips and frozen fingers for a bite to eat and a pit stop, all full of enthusiasm. In junior high he played for the Celtics, and we called them the "Green Machine." They had a great coach and did very well. Even though he didn't have the height for a vertical game, he was becoming a very aggressive point guard. At Oak Hill Academy in Virginia—that's where they teach discipline, how to study, and how to play basketball like Michael Jordan—he started looking like Bobby Hurley, a stellar point guard for Duke. We filmed one of his games. There was definitely a rhythm in the quick stops and starts and turns. He never lost the ball or the objective as he moved up and down the court against taller obstacles. He had choreographed it all and honed it to perfection. It was a joy to watch, so it was only natural that I got hooked on ACC basketball.

If you grow up in the south you inherently know that ACC is the only *real* basketball in existence, and it's a lot more satisfying than grits, which most outsiders automatically associate with "the South." I think the ACC is to basketball what the University of Virginia is to academia below the Mason-Dixon line. You just know UVA must be an incredibly terrific school because they have those upscale snooty window decals that simply state, "*The* University." And those decals are only allowed on cars that cost more than your mortgage, so if you happen to be from, say, South Dakota—God forbid—and don't know *which* university they're talking about, the implication is you have no business in the same hemisphere with a Mercedes. On top of that, you're probably driving a rusted out Volkswagen left over from the '60s.

A bumper sticker I've grown up on says it all about the ACC, and it poses that eternally perplexing question, "If God's Not a Tar Heel, Why Is the Sky Carolina Blue?" The answer is a dead giveaway, and everyone generally scores well on this quiz. I always aced this one because I believe there are a few eternal truths in this world, and one of them is Carolina basketball, Dean Smith, and now, Roy Williams. You can imagine how appalled I was to learn there are some ACC fans who actually dislike Carolina, but the majority of those are in therapy. Those cretins probably haven't looked at the sky since they were kids, much less noticed the color, and they don't know the difference between Tuesday and Saturday night. I think you are supposed to pray for people like that.

In terms of Dean Smith and Roy Williams, I've worked up my own Most Admired Person List over the past few years, and so far it hasn't failed me. My male list goes like this:

God

Jesus

FDR

Dean Smith

Roy Williams

This is a great list that is especially effective with Duke and Clemson fans, as well as Republicans and agnostics. My female list starts with Mother Teresa because you have to start with her, and it includes Eleanor Roosevelt, Gloria Steinem, Shirley MacLaine, and Bette Midler. This list has always worked for me.

Some years back I read in the paper that Florida State's Sam Cassell called the Tar Heel basketball fans a "wine and cheese crowd," all laid back. Since Florida State at that time had only recently joined the ACC, you couldn't expect them to understand the mentality overnight. That comes with maturity. Carolina fans are stark raving mad by most normal standards and can hardly be described as a no-sweat audience. They are commonly known as "Carolina Crazies," and they call themselves and each other that because it's a supreme accolade. For example, I personally knew a young couple, both students at Chapel Hill, who gave up meat with their meals the first semester of their married year together so they could buy season tickets to Carolina basketball games. I also know someone who purchased an entire house with only one bathroom because the built-in sun porch featured the UNC ram on a "Carolina Blue" wall. This guy is now a judge, all of his children graduated from Carolina, and I'm sure his grandchildren will as well. This man clearly has his priorities straight, and I'm trying to give Sam Cassell the benefit of the doubt here.

In order to properly appreciate February and the March Madness that follows in the ACC, you should be aware of the greatest rivalry in the galaxy. This rivalry makes Cain and Abel and the Hatfields and McCoys look like kids' stuff, and the warring factions of Romeo and Juliet's families, although intense, didn't happen just down "Tobacco Road" from each other. (Of course not. They lived in Verona, Italy.) You think Luke Skywalker had it in for Darth Vader? Get a grip! I'm talking about the mother of all rivalries in this highly unbiased account, and *the archri-vals* in basketball are The University of North Carolina, which God smiles upon, and Duke University, pronounced and spelled "Dook," which has a blue devil to symbolize its evil empire. If you're new at this, this is all you need to know. You don't need to watch any other basketball because the ACC has it all, and when those two mix it up on the court, it is cataclysmic, not to mention the fans who are all nuts. This is a good thing.

Other rivalries in basketball, especially outside this conference, remind me of two fleas fighting over a dog. I mean, who cares? Dook has a coach whose name is so hard to pronounce everybody just calls him "Coach K." out of frustration. Right there UNC has an edge because who can't pronounce Williams or Smith? So for those who are novices, there are two basic rules that are very important:

1. Never hire a coach whose name you can't pronounce.

2. "Dook" is vile and evil, and they must be destroyed.

That is extremely important to remember. Other hot tips about watching a Carolina/Dook game on TV: Time your trips to the bathroom, and work out your strategy. If Carolina is beating the evil empire with you there watching every move of the game, they are absorbing your positive energy through TV molecules, so you better stay right where you are. However, if they're in a brief slump, get to the bathroom or somewhere, whether you want to or not. Either that, or get very busy doing something in the same room, but don't peek and don't listen, because the molecules are quite perceptive, and that is transmitted to the UNC players. If they are really messing up, albeit briefly, you can help them pull it out by being "the devil's advocate," in this case, the Dook Blue Devils. That really works at times, and although it hurts to do it, you've got to yell very strongly worded statements at your television like: "Carolina, you suck!" and "How much do you want to lose this game?" and "Do you plan to hang around for the second half, or are you going home early?" The molecules transmit that energy, and the Tar Heel players start to worry. It's one thing to incur the wrath of a great coach, and that's powerful, but when the fans start beaming ugly thoughts, that's scary. Occasionally it produces good results, so every now and then you've got to pull out some *tough love!*

My daughter, who graduated with honors from UNC, and my son, who introduced me to basketball, have taught me a lot, but they never told me about this. This one I had to learn on my own: The main thing to remember about the ACC is always hedge your bets. No matter how well you know the teams' track records or the coaches' general strategies, and no matter how well you may have predicted outcomes in the past, it always pays to say, "On any given day in the ACC there can be a real upset," or something along those lines. Believe me, it can save you lots of money.

IF IT'S CLOSE TO EASTER, UNCLE SAM WANTS YOU

When Easter approaches on the Outer Banks, you know "the season" is about to break loose again. The weather starts warming up, and they are selling Easter baskets with all the trimmings off the shelves at every store. Everyone starts anticipating summer days on the beach, and it's about then that you realize the filing deadline for taxes is April 15. This is a universal headache that leads me to wonder who invented the calendar in the first place. Did they create it just to let you know you had to pay money to an entity that didn't earn it? "No, thank you. I think I'll keep my money this year." Next thing you know you wake up bruised and bloody in a cellblock down the hall from Hannibal Cannibal.

It is helpful to know up front that the most powerful forces in the universe are the IRS and insurance companies, in that order. Either category by itself is more powerful than the president, Congress, and the Supreme Court combined. Either category is more powerful than the stock market on a good day, the richest NBA player, all of the cruise missiles in the stratosphere, or the chairman of the federal reserve.

Neither Bill Gates nor Warren Buffet (or even Jimmy Buffet) can touch this crowd, so we are talking serious power and very deep pockets. As we know, Ben Franklin summed up this concept best when he said, "Nothing is certain but death and taxes."

Insurance companies know all about death because they count on it. Life insurance companies have tons of statistics about height and weight and age to the point you would think they were designing women's hosiery with the little charts on the back that advise you to buy petite, medium, large, or queen.

Health insurance companies make sure you die, and they virtually ensure it will be a long and painful death because they never pay out what you paid in, even though you took your life savings to do it. HMOs are a hybrid of this abnormality and probably worse.

Since health insurance is priced for the rich and famous and not poor peons like us, I thought we'd address another personal favorite: property insurance. When you own property, especially in a coastal community, you quickly realize these helpful companies do insure homes and all sorts of damage. That's right on the front of the policy in big letters. (It's wise to get a magnifying glass for the back of the policy, as well as the pages of disclaimers that follow, all drawn up by F. Lee Bailey.) So you pay the premiums because you thought all along they were insuring *your* house! It's my understanding a number of Katrina victims thought the same thing.

We've since learned they've streamlined this insurance business and put them all under one umbrella: FEMA. They have a handy toll-free number with lengthy menus in both English and Spanish, and that is: 1–888-RIP-U-OFF.

After all is said and done, the baddest guy on the block is the IRS, the most powerful invincible force in the galaxy. They have been around since day one, and if you doubt this, do remember why Mary and Joseph traveled to Bethlehem in the first place. It was to pay taxes, which I'm sure was not in their plans with Mary in her third trimester of pregnancy. Any woman who has ever had a child knows that a long distance haul, be it a Toyota or a donkey, at that point will probably bring on labor. All considered, Mary was lucky to make it to Bethlehem. Women know this, and it was all the IRS's fault, even though they traded under a different name in those days.

And the IRS will be here through infinity. If the universe destroys itself, either with the Big Bang or hair spray in the ozone layer, all the surviving cockroaches and jelly-doobers in petri dishes will get a

1040 form, which will have to be filled out and mailed in by a date written in blood, unless of course, they get an extension form.

Meanwhile, did you really think "Uncle Sam wants you" when you saw that face plastered on posters? That poster doesn't resemble any uncle I ever had. Get real! Uncle Sam doesn't want you. He wants your pocket, which is why his are deep and yours aren't. Did you really think any of the money you earned belonged to you?

Now that you are thoroughly armed with a background on the IRS, the following tax facts may be helpful. (Any material presented here is for general information only and should not be acted upon without further details and/or professional assistance.)

1. When you fill out your 1040 with personal information such as social security number, current address, and phone number, don't have your brother-in-law sign it.

2. Weapons of mass destruction, stealth bombers, cocaine, and Magnum .22s generally don't qualify for a tax write-off, no matter what line of work you're in.

3. If you declare a portion of your home for "business use," it's a good idea not to list the square footage of Nevada.

4. Tax exempt mileage is generally in the range of forty-plus cents per mile, depending on which tax year it is. We suggest you do not round up to $1.34 per mile, for example.

5. After a thorough review of our 1040s over several years, we realized the prize "standard deduction" generally goes to those who are (a) "married filing jointly," or (b) "qualifying widow/widower." You may want to pursue either, or both, of these options this tax year, preferably (a) before (b) because you may be able to double-dip that way, but we doubt it.

(If in doubt, get further details and/or professional assistance.)

Your 1040 normally allows credits for: child and dependent care, elderly or disabled care, adoptions, and foreign tax. In this regard, we suggest you not list your dog, cat, or rabbit under any of the first three categories—although if you have a dependent, disabled, elderly pet, you could try it. That seems reasonable to me.

Basic tax facts of life:

- The "Paperwork Reduction Act" isn't.
- "Short Forms" aren't.

If that weren't bad enough, we can't even take Excedrin as a tax write-off because these tax forms give us a headache. We have this on good authority from our tax professional.

NAGS HEAD
MEMORIES

In retrospect, I enjoyed the best part of my growing-up years at Nags Head after my parents built the cottage in the mid 1950s there among the old matriarchs at the waters' edge. The fire department later insisted on giving every cottage an address so they could find it in case of fire, but I only remember "something" Virginia Dare Trail. It was always the "Thirteen and a half milepost, you know, oceanfront, next door to Teeny's, not far from the post office and across the Beach Road from St. Andrews Church." Everybody gave directions like that, and no one had a problem finding anyone.

We first spent a week or so for several summers at the Dolphin Motel at the south end of the beach so my parents could look at any cottages for sale in that part of the beach. Dad knew all of the cottagers in the area, as well as many of the natives, because he'd spent his summers with them when he was young. It was still very much a family beach in those days, and many of the cottages had been passed from one generation to the next, a cherished tie to their past. I remember going to look at one of the old cottages with my parents, and my father never embarrassed me more. After we went through the inside, upstairs and down, he pulled out his pocketknife and shoved it into one of the floorboards of the front porch! It went in like butter and he concluded, "Nope, it's rotten."

So my parents built the three-bedroom, two-bath, smallish cottage high on pilings in the mid-1950s, right there among the "unpainted aristocracy," and that was fine because everybody welcomed another Old Nags Header and his family. I think I was about twelve or thirteen when they built Tern Cote, and I had three things against it from the beginning: everybody from my hometown went to "cool" beaches like Morehead or Atlantic Beach, *not* Nags Head. On top of that, they made me paint the major part of the inside of the cottage, and Mama had picked the color because it was quite "in" then. It was Holiday Turquoise, a lovely enamel paint which requires a lot of turpentine all over before you appear in public. To preface the perfect description of this delightful color, I'll just say I think the British are eloquent in their phraseology, and this is one I've never forgotten. When I was grown and married, my husband and I took our children to vacation there, as we always did, and one of his dearest friends from college and his British wife spent a couple of days with us. The first night they were there, we were sitting in the living/family room, and she said, "I say, I feel like I'm sitting in a fishbowl." My thought was, *Try painting the inside of a fishbowl!* Needless to say, my favorite color is *not* Holiday Turquoise to this day, and my brother also doesn't care for sanding floors that are later covered with linoleum, another "in" product of the '50s. They told him these activities were supposed to "build character," so when it comes to character, by all rights we should have it in spades.

But I digress. The third reason I grew to be really irritated with that place came into play when I was a teenager. I believe the fire department has since outlawed jalousie windows because they're impossible to get out of during a fire. More important, they are impossible to get out of at night when you want to sneak out to a party on the beach. Ann, my buddy next door, could always get out because they had sensible windows, and she had a ball, which I heard about the next day. Poor me.

It's funny how a place with all those drawbacks can hold so many fond memories. When I was growing up, I heard the best bedtime stories in the world that always began "When I was a little boy at Nags Head…" As I got older, some of the history became more and more fascinating, and I once asked my dad if his parents' cottage was the one that originally belonged to Francis Nixon, a wealthy planter from Perquimans County who built one of the first oceanfronts in 1866. Dad's family is from Hertford, North Carolina, in Perquimans County. He was Tom Nixon, and in fact, he had a brother named Francis, and he told me we are definitely part of that family. However, he told me they were the "rich Tom Nixons," whereas our side of the same family was the "poor Tom Nixons." No joke! I heard that all my life when we visited Hertford, and that's what everybody called them to keep them straight, and they both knew it. Nobody was offended, particularly not the Tom Nixon cousins, who got along just fine. It was simply a means of identification.

For those of you who may now have the means to purchase oceanfront property, I expect you can appreciate a prime example of inflation at its finest. This from a wonderful book by Susan Byrum Rountree called *Nags Headers*, which was published in 2001. In 1855, an Elizabeth City doctor built an oceanfront cottage in Nags Head, but he didn't like not having his neighbors nearby, so he purchased fifty acres of oceanfront land for thirty dollars from the Midgett family, one of the oldest native families on the Outer Banks. He then sold it to the neighbors back home for a dollar a lot, and the whole crowd became neighbors next to the ocean as well. (In summary, I'd call that an excellent investment.)

I recall two other favorite stories that Dad told me, which illustrate ingenuity in true Old Nags Head style. In the chapter "Old Mr. Hollowell's Business Emporium," the store fronted the Beach Road when our cottage was built. It was huge and had been a hotel as well, but it was originally on the sound side with the long pier for the boat that docked there, bringing the cottagers and their household goods for the summer. As the oceanfront community grew, it became evident the "mountain had to be moved to Mohammed" to enhance business, and this was achieved with a number of logs and mules. I was told the logs worked as skids, and as soon as the mules pulled the building over one set of logs, they'd put the logs in front again and repeat the process until they got that behemoth to the Beach Road. I have no doubt the mules probably objected, but it all worked out in the end.

My favorite example of ingenuity is one that involved seagulls and car tires. When people had the early cars and drove to Oregon Inlet, there was a serious problem on one stretch of the road that blew out tires left and right. Along that stretch, the gulls would drop oysters onto the road from over- head to crack open the shells so they could get the contents, which was pretty smart on the gulls' part. If you've ever walked barefooted, even briefly, on oyster shells, you know they're quite sharp, and tires don't fare much better than feet. Nobody wanted to shoot "Jonathan Livingston," so this was an environmen- tally friendly solution. It should also be noted there were no formal meetings and no committees formed, but rather a few people got together and painted sil- houettes of seagulls on that stretch of pavement, and it worked just fine: No seagull worth his salt is going to drop his meal to another gull!

Dad had known the Midgetts since he was a kid, and they have that marvelous "hoi toide" native accent, which I love. Jethro Midgett Sr., a fisherman, used to put his dory[5] in the ocean to set his nets in front of our cottage. It was amazing to watch that sturdy boat shoved bow first right into the breakers, and he would retrieve his nets the next morning. Jethro often gave us some fish, usually blues, spot and croakers, but one time he caught some pompano and they were especially delicious. My dad and Jethro Sr. used to talk a lot there on the beach, and I couldn't wait to see what was in the nets that day. Jethro's wife, Miss Mattie, ran the store that fronted the Beach Road not far north of us. The store had been moved from the sound side after the storm of 1933 and Jethro Jr., who was closer to my dad's age, ran the fish market there. We shopped at the store for staples, and I have a lot of fond memories of that store and its proprietors, but this one stands out in my mind. We were there getting goods one day, and Miss Mattie told my mother: "You know, Margaret (everyone called her Meg, but Miss Mattie called her by her formal name), I've always wanted to run a liquor store." Everyone knew Miss Mattie was a teetotaler, so my mother was stunned and asked her why. Miss Mattie's response was, "I always thought the bottles were so pretty." Now that I consider this, I can see how a bottle of *Crown Royal* would be prettier than a can of Vienna sausage. Miss Mattie was a large woman, and she was usually wedged in her rocking chair, which made the wooden floorboards creak when she rocked. We weren't fooled by that because, if required, she would be out of that chair in a heartbeat filling an order for a customer who wasn't familiar with the lay of the land in the store.

The Ash Wednesday storm of March, 1962, devastated the Outer Banks, and our cottage, which had been about ten feet above the sand, was almost flush afterward, but we fared better than many around us. Miss Mattie didn't want to leave her store unattended, Ash Wednesday storm or not, but she was flown out by helicopter in spite of her protests. That was good, because after the water receded, the dirty watermark in the store was about six feet up the wall.

Those proud people have an incredible work ethic, and they are tough because they were forced to survive in a harsh environment. I still recall overhearing a conversation my dad was having with one of the old natives one day, and he said, "I cut his 'eoiys' out I did, Tom." I'd never heard of such a thing, so I asked my father that night if the guy really "cut his eyes out," and my dad replied, "If he said so, I expect he did." Wow. I'd say that constitutes a "bad eye day," which is considerably worse than a "bad hair day."

The beauty of that place was the fact that I could roam free with my friends once I achieved "roaming age" and got my chores done. That was allowed as long as I could swim and show up at home for any required meals and at dark. We loved to walk to the Nags Head pier about a mile north of the cottage, and I saved my allowance for the best treat of all, going to That's a Burger, which fronted the Beach

Road not far away. It was the best hamburger joint in the world, a little tiny place where they fixed my burger and handed it through the screen window so I could eat with my buddies on one of the picnic tables in front.

That little roadside stand never heard of the trans fat or saturated fat craze, and they could have cared less about the cholesterol, sodium, or carbohydrate level of those burgers, and they didn't do mushrooms on top. They just made the biggest best burger in the world, and they had all the regular condiments, plus they would melt cheddar cheese on top if I wanted it, and they had the softest rolls and the very finest French fries, plus all the ketchup I needed. I could tell it was the best burger because it was almost bigger than my mouth, and when I bit into it, it squished and the juices and grease ran down my chin and usually onto my clothes. That was, indeed, a burger!

I think the reason I appreciated that place, in addition to the fact the burgers were awesome, was the fact the guy at the screen window never asked how I wanted it, as in "rare, medium, or well done" because the guy in the back was the cook and I didn't tell him how to do his job. By today's standards, they might be considered a little slack because they just served tasty greasy beef, no soy protein or tofu mixed in. Their hamburger rolls weren't baked "in house" from multiple grains of organic wheat products topped with multiple organic seeds from all over the world because Nags Head wasn't Hong Kong. Nor did they have any sun-dried tomatoes, arugula, or mushrooms on those burgers, be the mushrooms Porcini, Portobello, or shiitake, no matter how I like to drop the ending of the last one and go around saying it for fun. Nope, the guy at the screen took my order and my money, and it wouldn't take long to get my burger, fries, and a cold Coke. Then he'd slam the screen shut to keep the flies out and the cooking in.

One of the best adventures of all was climbing Jockey's Ridge and flying down on a big piece of cardboard or a flat trashcan lid. The steepest side then was the back of the ridge, and that was one spectacular ride. Jockey's Ridge was Mount Olympus, and I was a god on top, could almost see to Africa, or at least I thought so. The view at night was spectacular because there were lit-up fishing boats, as well as ships that were in the shipping lanes at sea, and when I looked down, the cars snaking around the base of the ridge on the bypass looked like a trail of well-trained fireflies. Jockey's Ridge is an experience in itself, and as much a part of Nags Head as the ocean. The sand shifts constantly, depending on the direction of the prevailing winds, and it would never stay where it had been my last time there, no matter how I told it to stay put.

Near the base of Jockey's Ridge was one of my favorite teenage memories, the Casino. I dated guys who took me bowling on the ground floor, but the most fun was the slick wooden dance floor and the awesome music upstairs. I could almost see my reflection in the floor, and it stayed that way because we were all required to check our shoes when we got upstairs. Barefoot dancing is the best, and that was one happening place because they booked nationally known bands on a regular basis. The sounds pumping out of the huge upstairs windows inspired many in the surrounding area. There were no screens in the windows; I suspect because there wasn't room for a fly to wedge into the crowd, but every now and then a serious partygoer would fall out of an upstairs window. The fall was usually broken by one of the cars parked below, but I don't recall anyone ever being seriously hurt, nor did they normally feel it when it happened. When I entered the dance floor upstairs, my wrist was stamped once they determined that I wasn't "underage." That stamp was invisible except under a black light, which the staff checked occasionally. I mainly knew when I got there that I was going to have a ball, and they never disappointed.

Years later I saw a woman at Ace Hardware, and she had on one of the rattiest T-shirts I'd ever seen. It had several holes in it and the colors were faded, but I could still see the picture of the Casino on the back. I went directly over to her and said, "I *want* your T-shirt." We had a wonderful talk for quite some time, and when I got home from the hardware store, I realized I hadn't bought anything even though I knew I'd gone for a reason. (Didn't I say earlier that I always have to make more than one trip to the hardware store?)

The Casino was quite a landmark and lasted for about forty years, until it was torn down. Donnie Twyne, the sheriff of Nags Head, often helped keep things under control there, but I never saw him, or if I did I didn't know who he was. Maybe he wore a disguise and it took a black light to see him too. I just know he struck fear in the hearts and minds of teenagers, and rumor was he'd arrested, or at least threatened, a group of teens for spitting watermelon seeds into the sand at Jockey's Ridge. Talk about the long arm of the law!

As a teenager, I automatically assumed beaches had tar on them because everybody got tar on their feet in Nags Head then. If I had a light-colored bathing suit, or especially a white one, I would absolutely get tar on it. It was amazing because I never got tar on a black bathing suit, but everyone had a bottle of kerosene and rag close by for tar removal. At that age, I decided it must be a natural beach phenomenon. I only learned later it was a situation that resulted from the Germans being rather successful at blowing up our ships just off the coast during World War Two. There's virtually no tar on the beaches now, only greedy developers, and I can't use tar on them, because Donnie Twyne could get me in the end!

My dad later installed central HVAC in the cottage, but we didn't have it then, and that was fine because there was a ceiling fan in every room and usually a wonderful breeze. But there's always an exception, and that was the five-day period when there was no breeze; it was humid and sticky, and the temperatures hovered in the upper nineties. Even the ocean was warm and yucky. Thankfully, Food Lion in Nags Head had been built, and it was amazing how all the neighbors hung out there over the freezer cases, admiring boxes of broccoli and cauliflower, even frozen bait. Nobody seemed to be buying much, but they were sure admiring the freezer contents.

Along the same lines, everyone had telephones and TVs at home, but few people had them in Nags Head then. Why have them when we had it all without them? This changed gradually, and at one point we did have a telephone, but no TV, which resulted in an interesting situation. My parents were next door at a porch party, and I was close enough to the cottage to hear the phone ring, so I got it. It was one of their friends from home, calling to warn us of a hurricane barreling straight toward the Outer Banks, which no one knew anything about. Someone found a television, and it was confirmed. I have never seen a crowd batten down the hatches and get out as fast. Shortly after that, my parents got a television for the cottage.

I realize how people say something "couldn't happen in a million years," but it does. Winning the lottery won't, but fishhooks can, or they certainly could in that environment. We'd come in for lunch after fishing out front, so we propped our rods on the railing of the high front porch, as we often did. This hadn't presented a problem before, but after lunch Dad was working on the cottage just below and one of the fishhooks lodged firmly in his head. He tried to get it out, but it wouldn't budge, plus his hair was matted with blood. He said it was numb, didn't hurt a bit, but he needed to get it out, and there was no emergency room in Nags Head then. He put on a baseball cap and drove to Manteo to get the doctor there to remove it. This would have been totally standard, except for something hilarious that occurred along the way. In Manteo the "hookee" knew he was in the general area of the doctor's office, so he asked a kid on the sidewalk for directions. When he took off the baseball cap to mop his brow, that poor child spotted the fishhook with some line attached, and he mainly saw the blood. He screamed at the top of his lungs and took off. The doctor removed the hook, gave Dad a shot, and he returned to the cottage all fixed up.

A child's perception can be quite different from that of an adult, and the second example was one I observed in a Kitty Hawk restaurant. I will preface this by saying, for those of you who haven't discovered the soft-shell crab, if you try one, you're in for a real treat. Much admired, the "softie" is greatly anticipated, the grandest delicacy, the "truffle" of the Outer Banks. However, the child I observed standing in his parents' booth, watching a woman eating a soft-shell crab sandwich, didn't seem to share this view. From his perspective, he saw little fried legs dangling out of a bun with the juices dripping. I'm sure the image wasn't helped by the fact that the fingers holding the sandwich had blood-red nails, and her teeth were gnashing into this helpless creature. The look on his face resembled the look you might imagine if someone put the Gerber baby in a blender! As I said, perceptions vary...

Throughout my youth and as an adult with children, I was committed to one cause, which was quite noble really. This is one my husband and our children shared, and we did it selflessly. We spent every minute we could on the beach, and it may have just looked like a frivolous pastime, but we were actually guarding the beach to prevent an invasion. After the Germans during World War Two and all the tar, we figured we couldn't be too careful. Our Patriotic Protection Program must have paid off because we were never invaded.

The final chapter is about the next generation, which is as it should be.

THE NEXT GENERATION

The children were introduced to Nags Head almost before they could walk, and they loved it. We all did. Case in point: my husband had two job offers, which were quite similar, except for location. It was an easy choice. We chose the one in Virginia Beach because it was an hour and a half drive to the cottage in the days before the influx of visitors, and we went down on weekends and spent most of our vacations there when it wasn't occupied. He was an architect and designed and oversaw the construction of a pitch roof to replace the original flat one on the cottage. During the winter on weekends, we painted the Holiday Turquoise interior a more inviting earth tone, which got everybody out of the fishbowl at last! It was a labor of love.

It didn't matter the time of year, the children couldn't wait to go to Nags Head, and we lived at a beach. Almost as soon as we got over the bridge, they would scan the horizon for the first glimpse of the ocean to make sure it was still there, and when the car door opened, they would race to the water's edge to stick their toes in, even in the dead of winter.

My son's name is Aaron, and we had a delightful neighbor who played the guitar and made up a song that went, "Big A, little a, r-o-n." I don't recall if it had any other words, but Aaron was an overnight sensation on our stretch of the beach, and people were always asking where "Big A, little a" was or how he was doing. Molly, the younger one, once crawled up her big brother's body the first time she spotted a sand crab, but she got over that quickly and has been quite independent ever sense. We had a genuine "salty dog," which was the name of a favorite cocktail at porch parties. Many people had a "salty dog," which is a dog that loves the ocean and shakes dry all over the nearest group of people, all full of happy dogness. That's expected, and nobody minded because we were wearing our bathing suits anyway.

The children naturally loved that wonderland. The Easter Bunny went to Nags Head, the tooth fairy was on call, and it's the best place in the world to swim, fly a kite, slide down a larger-than-life sand dune, climb the stairs of a lighthouse, or check out the catch of the day at Oregon Inlet when the charter boats come in. *The Lost Colony* speaks to all generations, especially with scary Indians in an outdoor theater next to Roanoke Sound. They seemed to think TV was "pretty crummy" for a while, after seeing real live people on stage and around them instead of being confined to a screen in a box, no matter the color quality or size of the screen.

The replica of the Wright Brothers' plane at the National Memorial in Kill Devil Hills was a symbol of the twelve-second flight in December of 1903, which changed history and technology forever. As I said, perceptions are often different in the mind of a child, and they were too young when we first took them. "That looks sorta flimsy. Why didn't they build a jet instead?" I don't recall, but I hope one of us explained that you have to learn to crawl before you stand up and walk.

We took them back when they were older. And as they got older, we took their friends down too, and it was safe enough for them to walk to the pier or the small shopping center across the Beach Road, even Jockey's Ridge. They both learned to swim when they were quite young, and there was a lot of surfing and boogie-boarding going on in front of the cottage, which is as it should be. And they learned the mantra I was taught, "No matter what, never sell the cottage. Keep it in the family, and pass it on to the next generation." I believed that, and so did they.

Their first flying experience was years later when I rented a flight on one of the small tour planes that provide a bird's-eye view of the Outer Banks. The children were older then, but frightened at first when they realized we left the ground. Shortly after they realized we weren't going to fall back down, they started looking at the scenery below from a perspective they'd never had, and they were absolutely exhilarated in a way I'd never seen. *Wow, Orville and Wilbur Wright, you had the vision to let us all be a bird and soar, if only for a brief while.* What visionaries!

The porch parties were a way of life there, and the kids were welcomed with soft drinks and snacks when they buzzed in and out. After a day on the beach, this was mainly a gathering on someone's porch to enjoy some great food, conversation, and a few drinks. Then everyone went home and had dinner. The invitation to these parties was quite informal, as in, when we were hosting one we ran up the "cocktail flag." A number of cottage owners had professionally made "cocktail flags" that they ran up the pole if the party was on their porch. The motifs ran the gamut from fish swimming in a cocktail glass to one my husband and I created for my parents. I came up with the motif that was indigenous to Nags Head; he drew it and made the templates, and I sewed it. It was the Nags Head Nag, with a keg instead of a lantern under his neck, and his expression looked a tad blurry, plus he had bubbles over his head. Unfortunately, we hadn't yet updated the fishbowl turquoise to an acceptable, inviting earth color, so that poor nag was saddled with a Holiday Turquoise background on the flag.

That was the James Bond era, even at the beach, and our next-door neighbor actually named his cat Pussy Galore after seeing *Goldfinger*. The James

Bond fascination came full circle when I was making lunch one day during summer vacation. The children decided that was a good time to fight constantly under the cottage, out of my reach. No matter how I threatened, it continued, so I called their father in from the beach and strongly suggested he "take care of it." He did indeed, and he told them in no uncertain terms that if they didn't stop, he would tie each one to a piling under the cottage facing each other all afternoon while we enjoyed the beach. Molly, four and a half years younger than her brother, immediately yelled. "With *A View to a Kill!*" We all cracked up laughing and spent the afternoon on the beach.

• • •

Unfortunately, my father sold the cottage in the mid-1990s, so it wasn't passed down through the family after all. I think my children were even more disappointed than I. In retrospect, we were fortunate to have it when we did because that haven had a magical impact on many lives. We were blessed to once have it as the best "home" of all, that sandy side of heaven.

ENDNOTES

1.   "Manteo to Murphy" is a reference to two towns at opposite ends of a very wide state. At one time there was a small sign posted in Manteo as you headed west: "Murphy, 543 Miles."

2.   This account is derived from a letter my father wrote, which described life on the Outer Banks during the 1920s and very early 1930s.

3.   It was officially known as "Mr. Hollowell's Store," but my dad dubbed this multiple purpose enterprise a "business emporium."

4.   This title is a take-off on an ancient computer program, "Lotus 1–2-3."

5.   A flat-bottomed boat with high sides and a sharp V-shaped bow.